WORKING WITH SELF-HARM AND SUICIDAL BEHAVIOUR

Working with Self-Harm and Suicidal Behaviour

Louise Doyle, Brian Keogh and Jean Morrissey

 macmillan education palgrave

First published 2015 by
PALGRAVE

Palgrave in the UK is an imprint of Macmillan Publishers Limited, registered in England, company number 785998, of 4 Crinan Street, London N1 9XW.

Palgrave Macmillan in the US is a division of St Martin's Press LLC, 175 Fifth Avenue, New York, NY 10010.

Palgrave is a global imprint of the above companies and is represented throughout the world.

Palgrave® and Macmillan® are registered trademarks in the United States, the United Kingdom, Europe and other countries.

ISBN 978–0–230–28367–1

This book is printed on paper suitable for recycling and made from fully managed and sustained forest sources. Logging, pulping and manufacturing processes are expected to conform to the environmental regulations of the country of origin.

A catalogue record for this book is available from the British Library.

A catalog record for this book is available from the Library of Congress.

Printed in China

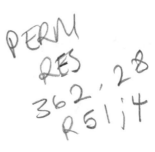

Contents

List of Figures and Tables

Figures

Tables

Acknowledgements

The authors and publisher would like to thank the following individuals and organisations for permission to reproduce copyright material:

Console for permission to reproduce material from the National Office for Suicide Prevention and Turas le Cheile (2012).

Samaritans for permission to reproduce material from *Help When We Needed It Most – How to Prepare and Respond to Suicide in Schools* (2013).

Time to Change for permission to reproduce the Time to Change tips card.

Introduction

Louise Doyle, Brian Keogh and Jean Morrissey

Suicide is a major public health problem worldwide accounting for almost one million deaths annually and a projected 1.5 million deaths annually by the year 2020. Non-fatal suicidal acts and other acts of self-harm occur much more frequently than completed suicide with most acts of self-harm hidden in the community never coming to the attention of mental health professionals. The extent of distress caused by both suicide and self-harm is clearly enormous. Completed suicide has a devastating and long-lasting effect leaving families, friends and communities distraught as they try to come to terms with their significant loss. Similarly, self-harm can impact hugely on families, friends and in the case of adolescents – school staff – who all struggle to understand the meaning of self-harm and may fear escalation of the self-harm behaviour to a suicidal act.

Suicide and self-harm prevention and reduction are priorities for those working in mental health and associated services, and this book serves as a useful resource for both students and practitioners in the fields of nursing, social work, occupational therapy and other health and social care professions. However, many people who die by suicide or engage in self-harm have no contact with the health service; therefore, people working in a wide array of different sectors need to be engaged in learning how to understand self-harm and suicidal behaviour and to respond appropriately to the needs of people at risk. This includes workers in the education sector, social services, the prison service, the voluntary sector and the media. Consequently, this book is also aimed at people working in these sectors who do not have a background in mental health and do not have an in-depth understanding of suicide and self-harm. While it may never be possible to *completely* understand suicide and self-harm, it is hoped that this text will assist in the endeavour to more fully comprehend these phenomena. It is an accessible text and was therefore purposively not laden with heavy academic or clinical terms that are not widely understood outside the realm of mental health. Instead, it is presented in such a way to make it useful for the teacher working with a pupil who self-harms, the prison officer working with a prisoner who has attempted suicide and the voluntary worker engaging with a client who has been bereaved by suicide. In an attempt to apply knowledge to real-life scenarios, case scenarios are presented in many chapters depicting examples of self-harm and suicidal behaviour in different contexts. Each chapter also has reflective questions which provide the reader with the opportunity to consolidate the knowledge they have gained from this text as they consider the questions asked.

Suicide and, in particular, self-harm evoke a range of negative attitudes and pejorative views from many people. It is important therefore to briefly consider this issue before progressing further in this text. A positive attitude towards those who engage in self-harm and suicidal behaviour and their families and friends is crucial to achieving any meaningful interaction with them. Many negative stereotypes are associated with people who self-harm and these often interfere with our ability to see the person and the reasons that they have engaged in self-harm on an individual level. Stereotypes work by grouping together large numbers of heterogeneous individuals and applying similar traits and characteristics to them. For example, the belief that people who engage in self-harming behaviour are 'attention seeking' will not achieve any positive outcome or help to address the problems inherent to the self-harming behaviour. In order to achieve a meaningful alliance or interaction, we need to be aware of our own attitudes, beliefs and prejudices so that they do not influence our behaviour. Key to achieving a positive outcome when working with people who self-harm is firstly education about suicide and self-harm, and secondly feeling equipped with the skills to communicate and intervene effectively. One of the aims of this book is to increase knowledge about suicide and self-harm and to provide strategies that can be used when working with this diverse group of individuals.

This book comprises of 10 chapters which offer key information about suicide and self-harm from a range of perspectives. Many of the chapters offer strategies that can be used when working with people who engage in self-harm and suicidal behaviour. In Chapter 1, drawing on the biological, psychological and socio-cultural perspectives, the reader will be introduced to the main theories that attempt to explain suicide and self-harm. The main aim of the chapter is to demonstrate how these theories aid our understanding of suicide and self-harm and how they impact on the approaches to the management and treatment of people who engage in suicide and self-harm. Chapter 2 examines stigma and suicide and self-harm. It defines stigma and looks at stigma-prevention strategies from a policy context. In addition it presents ways that individuals working with people who self-harm can prevent inadvertently stigmatising them. It also presents some strategies that may be useful for people who are affected by negative self-belief because of their suicidal feelings. Chapter 3 focuses on risk and protective factors for self-harm and suicidal behaviour. Throughout the literature many studies have tried to identify the predictors of self-harm and suicide from various theoretical perspectives; however, no universal model explains either phenomenon conclusively. The likelihood of a person engaging in self-harm or suicidal behaviour is influenced by a range of psychological, biological, social and environmental risk and protective factors. Identification of factors that may increase or decrease a person's level of risk can contribute towards the assessment of self-harm and/or suicide risk. This chapter, in an accessible way, presents commonly identified risk and protective factors and identifies more specific warning signs of imminent suicidal behaviour.

Patterns of self-harm and suicidal behaviour differ across the lifespan, with suicide peaking in adolescence/early adulthood and again in the older person while self-harm is predominately a feature of adolescence and early adulthood. The factors affecting a person's decision to harm themselves or deliberately end their life can change as they move from childhood through adolescence, adulthood and on to older age. Chapter 4 looks at each stage of life and discusses the specific issues that influence patterns of suicide and self-harm in childhood, adolescence, adulthood and older age. The emphasis in this chapter is on recognising age-specific factors which influence self-harm and suicidal behaviour.

Self-harm has received increasing awareness and attention among professionals, workers and lay persons, however little information or training is available, which enables people to understand and respond more skilfully and effectively to people who self-harm. Chapter 5 examines the nature of self-harm and addresses some of the issues involved from the perspective of those who are harming themselves, as well as the workers and helpers working in voluntary and community settings. Some guidance for addressing some of these issues will also be offered. There is increasing awareness of self-harm and suicide among professionals and lay persons alike, yet, at the same time, the interactions around self-harm and suicidal behaviour are often fraught with anxiety and confusion. Communication is a fundamental component of all therapeutic work and is paramount when working with people who self-harm and/or those who are at increased risk of suicide. The knowledge and interpersonal skills that the helper uses to communicate are essential aspects of carrying out a suicide risk assessment while at the same time facilitating the development of a positive helping relationship. Chapter 6 examines the verbal and non-verbal communication skills and interventions that are most relevant to undertaking a risk assessment and illustrates how each skill can be used in practice.

Working with people who are suicidal or who self-harm means being exposed to intense and extreme emotions. In a context of helping, the need for workers to pay attention to their own well-being is paramount not only for the sake of themselves but also for their clients and work colleagues. Chapter 7 examines the role of self-care and its use in a work/helping setting. Examples of various strategies that aim to help the worker identify his/her self-neglecting tendencies and to enhance their capacity to self-care are also outlined.

Preventing and reducing suicide and self-harm is an important public health target for most countries. In Chapter 8, we look at national and international prevention and reduction initiatives that are in place to reduce suicide and self-harm. Specific suicide and self-harm prevention and reduction initiatives are examined and the challenges of implementation of such initiatives considered. This chapter includes a consideration of both the general population approach to suicide and self-harm prevention and also the targeted approach incorporating specific 'at risk' groups. Included also is a consideration of some harm reduction approaches for those who repeatedly self-harm. Chapter 9 looks at the area of postvention and how we can assist those who are bereaved following the death of a loved one by suicide. The chapter discusses the concept of grief and complicated grief and presents some strategies for communicating with and assisting people in the days and weeks following bereavement. It also looks at the concept of peer support and the role of professional help during this difficult time. Finally, Chapter 10 looks at the issue of self-harm and suicide in three specific locations: prisons, school and emergency departments. In this chapter, there is a focus on preventing and responding to self-harm and suicide in these contexts.

This book is not intended to be a comprehensive text on suicide and self-harm. Rather it aims to increase basic understanding about both phenomena. Ultimately, we hope that this text proves an accessible and useful resource for those working either directly or indirectly with someone who is suicidal or self-harming, or for anyone who has an interest in the prevention of suicidal behaviour.

CHAPTER 1

Understanding Suicide and Self-Harm

Brian Keogh

Introduction

Drawing on biological, psychological and sociological perspectives, the purpose of this chapter is to introduce the reader to the main theories that attempt to explain suicide and self-harm. Biological perspectives will examine the role of age, gender, genetics as well as altered neurotransmitter functioning such as decreased serotonergic activity. Psychological components will briefly explore psychoanalytic theories and the role of interpersonal communication. Sociological perspectives will examine social integration and social regulation, drawing mainly from the work of Durkheim. It is acknowledged that this subject is very complex and that the information presented in this chapter is not exhaustive. Many other interpretations of suicide and self-harm are available within the extensive literature on the subject. In addition to introducing the theories, the chapter will provide examples of how they might inform our understanding of the subject. It will begin though by defining suicide and self-harm.

LEARNING OUTCOMES

By the end of this chapter, you should be better able to:

1. explain the complexities associated with defining suicide and self-harm;
2. outline the importance of having a theoretical understanding of suicide and self-harm;
3. differentiate between the biological, psychological and social approaches to understanding suicide and self-harm;
4. appreciate the importance of having an integrated approach to understanding suicide and self-harm.

Defining suicide and self-harm

According to O'Carroll et al. (1996: 246), the term 'suicide' refers to 'death from injury, poisoning, or suffocation, where there is evidence (either explicit or implicit) that the injury was self-inflicted and that the decedent intended to kill himself/herself'. However, other concepts related to suicide such as self-harm or attempted suicide are less clearly defined or understood. This has meant that they are often used interchangeably to mean the same thing and are value-laden resulting in negative perceptions of people who engage in them (Doyle, 2008). Because there is a strong correlation between self-harm and completed suicide, it is preferable therefore to conceptualise them as a continuum rather than as distinct entities. Although the numbers of people who engage in some form of self-harming behaviour are much higher than those who go on to complete suicide and they have varying levels of intent (from no intent to strong intent), they remain a very high-risk group. Many terms describe the spectrum of suicide and self-harm and suicidal behaviour, and some of them are listed in Box 1.1:

BOX 1.1   CONCEPTS ASSOCIATED WITH SUICIDE AND SELF-HARM

Suicidal Ideation: Thoughts about engaging in suicidal behaviour (O'Carroll et al., 1996).

Suicidal Intent: Actively considering a plan to die by suicide (Doyle, 2008).

Suicidal Threat: A verbal or non-verbal action that suggests that the individual might engage in suicidal behaviour in the future (O'Carroll et al., 1996).

Deliberate Self-Harm (DSH): The various methods by which people deliberately harm themselves, including self-cutting and taking overdoses. Varying degrees of suicidal intent can be present and sometimes there may not be any suicidal intent, although an increased risk of further suicidal behaviour is associated with all DSH (HSE et al., 2005).

Suicide Attempt: A potentially self-injurious behaviour for which there is evidence that the person intended at some level to kill himself/herself (O'Carroll et al., 1996: 247).

Non-Suicidal Self-Harm (NSSH): Now included as a distinct condition within The Diagnostic and Statistical Manual of Mental Disorders 5th Edition (DSM V), NSSH refers to self-harming behaviours not aimed at ending life (APA, 2013).

A theoretical understanding of suicide and self-harm

According to the Cambridge online dictionary, a theory can be defined as 'a formal statement of the rules on which a subject of study is based or of ideas that are suggested to explain a fact or event or, more generally, an opinion or explanation'. Theory tries to help us understand complicated concepts such as self-harm and suicide by attempting to explain why they occur. In addition, they influence how we care for and treat people who present with these problems. While there are many different perspectives and some of them will be touched on in this chapter, the three dominant theoretical perspectives are the biological, psychological and sociological approaches to understanding why suicide and self-harm occur. An overview of these three approaches is presented in Table 1.1

Suicide and self-harm have tended to fall within the biological interpretation of mental distress as an illness. This means that hospitalisation and the use of psychotropic drugs are the dominant strategies in terms of care and treatment. However, the rates of suicide and self-harm have steadily increased in the Western world, which suggests that social and psychological issues may be more influential over the individuals' biological or genetic profile. Furthermore, the often sudden and unexpected act of suicide may further suggest that psychological and social issues may be dominant. Confusion and lack of agreement about how suicide and self-harm are understood have led theorists to examine more integrated ways of approaching the subject. This is often articulated as a biopsychosocial approach, and it attempts to see suicide and self-harm not as having one explanation but several. This approach attempts to capture the complexity of suicide and self-harm by suggesting that there are many inter-related ways of understanding it. Therefore our understanding of suicide and self-harm can be drawn from biological, psychological and social perspectives.

Biological perspectives

The biological approach can be examined in two ways: firstly, as in the example earlier, it can be viewed in terms of structural, genetic or neurochemical influences that can contribute to suicide or self-harm. Secondly, components of our being, which we have no control over, can predispose us or increase our risk for suicide or self-harm. In this section, the main biological perspectives will be discussed briefly. It is important to reiterate here that the biological components should not be looked at in isolation and other factors, not just these alone, influence individuals' decision to engage in suicide and self-harm.

Gender and Age: A person's gender and age may predispose them to suicide and self-harm. While suicide across the lifespan is discussed in a later chapter of the book, the relationship with age and suicide and self-harm is discussed briefly here. According to the World Health Organisation, approximately 80% of the people who complete suicide each year are male. In the past, older men were more vulnerable to suicide; however, in recent times the rates among younger men (between the ages of 15 and 24) have increased making them the most vulnerable in some countries. In terms of worldwide figures for completed suicides, the highest rates are in men aged 70–79 years and in men over 80 years (Varnik, 2012). Suicide rates in women are lower in all countries except China where female deaths from suicide outnumber male deaths (Varnik, 2012). While women are overrepresented in terms of suicidal ideation and self-harm, they are less likely to die by suicide, a phenomenon described by Canetto and Sakinofsky (1998) as a gender paradox. For self-harm, while the age of onset is similar for men and women (early to mid-teens), the National Registry of Self Harm in Ireland (2012) found that rates of self-harm peak for

Table 1.1   Overview of the theoretical approaches to suicide and self-harm

Theoretical approach	Example	Influence on treatment approaches
Biological approach	Suggests that physical or structural problems can cause or contribute to suicide and self-harm. For example, a deficiency of the neurotransmitter serotonin is believed to cause depression which may lead to self-harm or suicide. Suicide and self-harm are often seen as an illness or disease.	Within the biological sphere, often the treatment revolves around the restoration of the deficient neurotransmitter (in this example, serotonin) usually through taking medications, especially anti-depressants.
Psychological approach	The psychological or psychodynamic approach attempts to move away from the idea of suicide and self-harm as an illness. Often they are seen as the result of struggles between mental processes or as a response to anxiety. In addition, suicide and self-harm can sometimes be viewed as responses to early childhood experiences.	The wide variety of interventions that are used within the psychological or psychodynamic sphere falls under the large umbrella of the 'talking therapies' or 'psychotherapies'. There are many different schools of thought on the nature of mental distress from this perspective, and this influences the type of therapy that is used. For example, traditional psychoanalysis emerged from Freud's work on the unconscious mind. Consequently, therapy focuses on the unconscious unresolved conflicts that are causing problems.
Sociological approach	The sociological perspective looks at the social determinants of health and illness and proposes that individuals' social circumstances are influential and can contribute to suicide and self-harm. For example, poverty, access to healthcare and education may lead to suicide and self-harm.	Interventions from a sociological perspective focus on improving communities in terms of health and mental health outcomes. This is achieved through mental health policy and practice, education, etc. For example, the fear of being stigmatised often prevents individuals from seeking help. Strategies to de-stigmatise mental distress may reduce the level of suicide and self-harm as individuals may access mental health services earlier.

males between the ages of 20 and 24 years, and gradually decrease thereafter. However, for women, the rates of self-harm peak at the age of 15–19 years, and they remain relatively constant into middle age (Griffin et al., 2013).

Genetics: The study of suicide and self-harm from a genetic point of view tends to consider family history, twin and adoption studies. According to Mann and Currier (2007), there is evidence that genetics plays a role in suicide and self-harm. Qin et al. (2003) found that a family history of suicide significantly increased suicide risk. However, a family history of suicidal behaviour may be explained by an increased genetic predisposition to mental health problems generally rather than suicide and self-harm specifically (Nock et al., 2012). In addition, Brent and Mann (2005) found in their review about adoption studies, that there was some evidence to suggest that the incidence of suicide among adoptees supported a genetic effect.

Altered Serotonergic Activity: According to Van Heeringen et al. (2004), the majority of biological research has concentrated on the role of the neurotransmitter serotonin. Neurotransmitters are chemical messengers that are responsible for communication at a biochemical level in our brain and throughout our body. Serotonin is one of these neurotransmitters, and it is believed to contribute to how we feel on an affective level (mood). Alterations in serotonin levels therefore are believed to impact negatively on our mood and our sense of well-being, resulting in depression and low mood. According to Opacka-Juffry (2008), the role of serotonin in contributing to depression has become widely acceptable, and there are many research studies to support this stance. However, serotonin's mode of action and its role in contributing to depression, suicide and self-harm is complex and not fully understood. For example, depression is a very common phenomenon, but not everyone who is depressed is suicidal or engages in self-harming behaviour. It may be that other neurotransmitters are involved as well as the person's social and psychological circumstances, which are influential in the decision-making process. Furthermore, many people who die from suicide are not known to be depressed from a clinical depression point of view, furthering the viewpoint that other factors within the social and psychological domains are important determinants in the decision to engage in self-harm or attempt suicide. Specific to self-harm, McGough (2012) suggests that the release of endorphins and adrenaline when the skin is cut may contribute to a sense of pleasure or excitement consequently perpetuating its use.

In summary, from a biological point of view, suicide and self-harm are generally believed to emerge from discrepancies in the transmission of serotonin, although other neurotransmitters are also believed to be involved. Factors like genetics, age and gender are fixed, so consequently, in terms of suicide prevention, an awareness of these factors coupled with additional support for people who are vulnerable from an age and gender point of view is an important preventative strategy. While the use of antidepressants may be helpful for people who are clinically depressed, this approach alone may not be suitable for all, given the diverse and often complex reasons that individuals engage in suicide and self-harm. Furthermore, aligning suicide and self-harm exclusively with biological interpretations of mental distress may inadvertently remove some of the responsibilities that individuals have when it comes to managing their own mental health.

Psychological perspectives

Sigmund Freud has often been cited as the father of modern psychoanalysis, and his influence on the wide variety of modern 'talking therapies' cannot be underestimated. Freud believed that unresolved conflicts that often occurred during childhood were subconsciously repressed and emerged later in life as mental distress. His approach to therapy was primarily concerned with rooting out and addressing the unresolved issues causing distress with techniques such as dream analysis and free association. In terms of suicide and self-harm, Freud's approach seeks to establish the unconscious and repressed experiences that occurred which emerge as suicidal ideas and self-harm. Freud believed that two instincts (life and death) were responsible for most human behaviour. In this section, three theories which attempt to specifically understand attempted suicide and suicide will be briefly examined:

1. Attempted suicide as a cry for help or a cry of pain;
2. Suicide caused by psychache;
3. Why people die by suicide.

In addition, some of the functions of self-harm, specifically from a psychological perspective, will be considered.

Attempted suicide as a cry for help or a cry of pain: Tabachnick and Farberow (1961: 63) adequately summarise the cry for help as being

> based on the consideration of self-destructive behaviour as a means of communicating to others various feelings and demands or pleas. The self-destructive behaviour thus becomes, in part, a communication with a particular purpose and content directed toward a specific audience.

Simply put, the cry for help attempts to explain attempted suicide as a form of interpersonal communication, where the individual engages in self-destructive behaviour in an attempt to receive some support or assistance from their social support network or from health professionals. Williams (1997: xii) compliments the cry for help theory by suggesting that prior to the individuals cry for help there is a cry of pain:

> Suicidal behaviour may be overtly communicative in a minority of cases, but mainly it is 'elicited' by the pain of a situation with which the person cannot cope – a cry of pain, and only then a cry for help.

Similar to psychache, which will be discussed later in this chapter, suicide and suicidal behaviour occur in response to an unbearable situation. While the cry for help theory assists us to understand the motives behind why some individuals engage in suicidal behaviour or attempt suicide, it has had a somewhat negative impact on some people. In some cases, it has led people to be labelled as 'manipulative' and 'attention seeking', meaning that they often get a negative reaction from the mental health services when they engage with them. This results in non-attendance at follow-up appointments or failure to engage with any form of services at all. The fact remains that many people who engage in self-harm or attempt suicide are at an increased risk of completing suicide and that a previous suicide attempt remains the largest risk factor for completing suicide in the future.

Suicide caused by psychache: The 'cry for help' understanding of suicide and suicide behaviour is not ideal as it does not explain why some people engage in self-harm and attempt suicide while a small proportion of these go on to complete suicide. Furthermore its utility rests primarily with understanding people whose motives is not to die. Consequently, understanding why someone decides to kill themselves is fundamental to preventative strategies. In addition, an understanding of why people who engage in non-lethal self-harm go on to die by suicide and what makes them move from one state of mind to the next is crucial. While a clear understanding of this might never be achieved and each person will have a number of interacting complex factors, Edwin Shneidman has attempted to articulate why individuals choose suicide. Shneidman has written extensively on the subject of suicide and to summarise his work here is beyond the scope of this chapter. Simply put, and in his own words, Shneidman (1999: 239) states that:

> Suicide is caused by psychache. Psychache refers to the hurt anguish, soreness, aching, psychological pain in the psych, the mind. It is intrinsically psychological – the pain of excessively felt shame, or guilt, or humiliation, or loneliness, or fear, or angst, or dread of growing old or of dying badly, or whatever. When it occurs, its reality is introspectively undeniable. Suicide occurs when the psychache is deemed by that person to be unbearable.

Shneidman (1996) explains that the goal of suicide is to find relief from psychache and to achieve a state of peace. In addition to psychache, a number of other factors need to be present:

- The person has a reduced threshold for psychological suffering and cannot bear the psychache (psychological pain).
- The person sees no escape from the psychache other than suicide.
- The person may or may not be experiencing depression (Shneidman, 1999).

Why people die by suicide: This theory presented by Thomas Joiner in 2005 attempts to explain suicide using a three-stage model. Joiner suggests that the desire to die must be coupled with the individual's ability to inflict harm to themselves which he believes is acquired over time. The desire to die is comprised of two psychological states, 'burdensomeness' and 'thwarted belongingness', which counteract conditions that are necessary for the will to live to remain intact – 'effectiveness' and 'connectedness' (Joiner, 2005).

Functions of self-harm

While more details about the characteristics of people who self-harm will be presented later in Chapter 3, it is useful at this point to examine briefly why individuals engage in self-harm as distinct from attempted suicide and suicide. However, it should be noted that self-harm may serve multiple psychological functions:

> *Affect Regulation*: Managing intense emotions such as anger, stress or anxiety is often cited as the most common reason that individuals engage in self-harm.
>
> *Self-Punishment*: Self-harm is sometimes seen as an attempt to self-punish the individual.
>
> *Interpersonal Influence*: Individuals may engage in self-harm in order to influence other people, for example to receive assistance or affection.
>
> *Anti-dissociation*: This relates to the infliction of self-harm as an act to arrest feelings of unreality or the sense that they feel nothing at all.
>
> *Anti-suicide*: In some cases, self-harm may be used to resist suicide attempts.
>
> *Sensation Seeking*: Self-harm may evoke a feeling of excitement or a high in some individuals.
>
> *Interpersonal Boundaries*: For some people, self-harm may help them remain more independent and in control (Klonsky & Muehlenkamp, 2007).

In summary, three different psychological theories have been described briefly here. Two concentrate on suicide while the other is more focused on attempted suicide. While some might argue that the two cannot be looked at in isolation to each other, when put together they do help to clarify and describe the range of psychological factors that are experienced by individuals who engage in suicide and attempted suicide. Some of the functions of self-harm have also been briefly presented as distinct from suicide and self-harm which help to demonstrate the differences between the concepts and illuminate their complexity.

Sociological perspectives

From a health perspective, sociology examines the role of social factors that can have a positive and negative impact on our health. For example, sociology often considers the role that education has on our health and might argue that those not afforded the opportunity of an education many be prone to poorer health. A lack of education often has the knock-on effect of leading to poorer employment prospects and consequently lowered incomes or unemployment, all of which negatively impact on health, including mental health. These factors are discussed in more detail in Chapter 3. One of the most well-known and enduring social theories, Durkheim's study on suicide, will be briefly discussed in this section. In addition, this section will briefly examine some of social factors that influence suicide and self-harm. The concept of social stigma is discussed in detail in Chapter 2.

Durkheim's theory on suicide: Durkheim developed his theory during the Industrial Revolution when there was a major change in how society was organised. Urban areas became more densely populated as the rural community sought employment and better prospects within cities and towns throughout Europe. Durkheim described what he called a social milieu where external forces influenced the actions and behaviours on the individuals within it. Within the social milieu, different people operated at different levels of social integration. Those individuals who had weak ties to their social milieu or lower levels of social integration were demonstrated to have higher rates of suicide among them (Thomson, 2006). Durkheim described these deaths as egoistic suicides. Conversely, individuals who had higher levels of social integration were also associated with a higher rate of suicide, and these were described as altruistic suicides as Durkheim believed that they were sacrifices for the good of the social milieu (Thomson, 2006). Durkheim described four different types of suicide, and each was characteristic of either modern urban societies or rural non-industrial societies. These are briefly explained in Table 1.2.

Table 1.2   Four types of suicide after Durkheim (Hyde et al., 2004)

Modern societies	**Egoistic suicide:** These occur because individuals have fewer ties with society and consequently have lower levels of social integration.
	Anomic suicide: These occur during times of major change (e.g. the Industrial Revolution) where society appears to fragment and become less regulated.
Rural societies	**Altruistic suicide:** These occur for the greater good, where individuals 'sacrifice' themselves for society. Result from high levels of social integration.
	Fatalistic suicide: These occur in societies that are very regulated, where the individual sees no other way to escape except by killing themselves.

Anomie

Durkheim (1952) popularised the concept of 'Anomie', a term he wrote about in his book called *Suicide: A Study in Sociology* and then later developed in his work 'The Division of Labour'. According to Thompson (2006: 424), anomie was 'Durkheim's term for the condition of modern society in which there were too few moral regulations as guides'. On one hand, anomie exists because at times of social change, the rules and regulations governing a society appear to diminish and levels of social integration similarly erode resulting in higher levels of suicide (Besnard, 1988; Fincham et al., 2011). On the other hand, society can be said to be in a constant state of change and that anomie emerges in response to constant change and the lack of stability in a modern world (Besnard, 1988). It could be argued that suicide has increased over time not in response to abrupt changes in social systems but because, as Besnard (1988: 92) suggests, of the pressure on individuals 'to advance constantly towards an indefinite goal'.

While Durkheim's theories on suicide were written over 100 years ago, they still have relevance today in terms of how we understand suicide from a sociological perspective. In modern times, as communities have become less cohesive, there has been an increase in suicide. Likewise, the increase in a more secular society has also been associated with growth in the numbers of people who are taking their own lives. This perhaps is influenced by the lack of unity that is often associated with belonging to a religious organisation. In addition, faith, in a general sense, provides a protective buffer to suicide. During times of economic crisis such as a recession, levels of unemployment increase consequently increasing the social pressures on individual not only in terms of financial burden but also in terms of eroding societal roles and negatively impacting on the levels of social integration that employment fulfils. As noted earlier, the levels of suicide increase as people get older; it could be argued that some of these are altruistic suicides, as older people die by suicide to avoid being a burden on their families. Many of these issues are rooted in societal values and norms, and a sense of marginalisation or being perceived as being an outsider can make individuals vulnerable to suicide. In addition, the presence of a mental health problem also increases vulnerability to engaging in suicidal behaviour. Other factors can serve as a buffer to suicide, for example, being married or being in a steady relationship can offer some protection against suicide. These risk and protective factors will be explored in more detail in Chapter 4.

From a sociological perspective, self-harm has increased in the Western world in recent years, and phenomena such as the media and the Internet may be influential in the rise in number of people who are harming themselves. Other factors such as bullying in schools may also leave younger people feel that they have no other alternative except to engage in self-harm, and this may be linked to their individual coping mechanisms which will be discussed briefly in the next section. Individual's support networks, such as friends and family, are also influential, for example their perception of the support that is available to them to cope with stressors. In addition, Senker (2013) suggests that being part of a clique where self-harm is practised and the resultant peer pressure may also contribute to incidents of self-harm.

Stress, suicide and self-harm

The final perspective that will be examined in this chapter is the role of stress and, in particular, how people react and cope with stress in terms of suicide and self-harm. Many models of stress and coping have been proposed, and the most commonly discussed is that of Lazarus and Folkman (1984). Coping according to Lazarus and Folkman (1984) refers to behavioural and cognitive efforts to deal with demands that are perceived as stressful and beyond the resources of the individual. They describe two types of coping:

1. Emotional focused coping attempts to lessen stress through either minimising the impact of the stressor or avoidance.
2. Problem focused coping attempts to manage stress through effective problem solving such as defining the problem and generating a range of possible solutions.

Central to these types of coping is the individual's perception of the situation or event as stressful. This appraisal of the stressor is also contingent with the internal and external resources that are available to them to cope. Individuals who are faced with a stress that is beyond their perceptions of what they can control and who also feel that they do not have the resources to manage this stress may be vulnerable to suicide and self-harm. On the other hand, those who use alcohol or drugs to cope with stressors may also be at risk. Many individuals who engage in self-harm often do so under the influence of alcohol or drugs, suggesting that individual's ability to cope with stress is reduced during periods of intoxication, therefore worsening episodes of self-harm. Another model called the stress diathesis model has also been proposed. In this model, it is suggested that individuals are vulnerable to suicide and self-harm because they are predisposed to greater and more severe reactions to stress. Here it is argued that individuals who display, for example, cognitive rigidity (difficulty relating to other people's point of view) or dichotomous thinking (black and white thinking) are vulnerable to suicide and self-harm because these characteristics interfere with their problem-solving abilities when they are faced with life stress (O'Connor & Sheehy, 2000).

Conclusion: An integrated approach to understanding suicide and self-harm

The aim of this chapter was to introduce the reader to some of the main reasons why individuals complete suicide or engage in self-harm. In that sense, the main biological, psychological and social explanations have been briefly presented independently to each other. On their own, when presented separately, they may appear to offer quite simple explanations to behaviour that is incredibly complex. For that reason, it is important to think about the models presented here as being integrated so that no one factor is seen as the reason for a person to attempt or complete suicide or engage in self-harm. For example, significant stressful life events are often cited as the reasons that people die by suicide However, many people experience life stress but do not engage in suicide or self-harm. For many people bereaved by suicide, there is no clear explanation for why their loved ones took their own life. The theories when understood in an integrated way help us to understand the complexity of the concepts associated with suicide and self-harm while assisting researchers and clinicians in developing and implementing prevention and treatment options.

REFLECTIVE QUESTIONS

1. How does having a biological, psychological and sociological understanding of suicide and self-harm help you to explain why suicide and self-harm occurs?
2. A number of sociological determinants of mental health have been discussed in this chapter. Which ones do you think are important in suicide prevention and self-harm?
3. What do you understand by the terms suicidal ideation and intent? Give examples to illustrate your answer.
4. What theoretical perspective would you like to learn more about and for what reasons?

REFERENCES

American Psychiatric Association. (2013) *Diagnostic and Statistical Manual of Mental Disorders, Fifth Edition (DSM-5)*. Arlington: American Psychiatric Publishing.

Besnard, P. (1988) The true nature of anomie. *Sociological Theory,* 6(1): 910–995.

Brent, D. and Mann, J. (2005) Family genetic studies, suicide, and suicidal behaviour. *American Journal of Medical Genetics Part C,* 133C(1): 13–24.

Canetto, S. and Sakinofsky, I. (1998) The gender paradox in suicide. *Suicide and Life-Threatening Behavior,* 28(1): 1–23.

Doyle, L. (2008) Care of the person with suicidal behaviour. In Morrissey, J., Keogh, B. and Doyle, L. (eds.) *Psychiatric/Mental Health Nursing: An Irish Perspective*. Dublin: Gill & Macmillan Publishing, pp 222–236.

Durkheim, E. (1952) *Suicide: A Study in Sociology*. Oxfordshire: Routledge Classics.

Fincham, B., Langer, S., Scourfield, J. and Shiner, M. (2011) *Understanding Suicide: A Sociological Autopsy*. London: Palgrave Macmillan.

Griffin, E., Arensman, E., Wall, A., Corcoran, P. and Perry, I.J. (2013). *National Registry of Deliberate Self-Harm Annual Report 2012*. Cork: National Suicide Research Foundation.

Health Service Executive. (2005) *National Office for Suicide Prevention Annual Report*. Dublin: HSE.

Hyde, H., Lohan, M. and McDonnell, O. (2004) *Sociology for Health Professionals in Ireland*. Dublin: Institute of Public Administration.

Joiner, T. (2005) *Why People Die by Suicide*. Cambridge: Harvard University Press.

Klonsky, E.D. and Muehlenkamp, J.J. (2007) Self-injury. A research review for the practitioner. *Journal of Clinical Psychology*. 63: 1045–1056.

Lazarus, R. and Folkman, S. (1984) *Stress Appraisal and Coping*. New York: Singer Publishing Company.

Mann, J. and Currier, D. (2007) A review of prospective studies of biologic predictors of suicidal behaviour in mood disorders. *Archives of Suicide Research* 11(1): 3–16.

McGough, G. (2012) *Self Harm: The Essential Guide*. Peterborough: Need 2 Know.

Nock, M., Borges, G., Bromet, E., Cha, C., Kessler, R. and Lee S. (2012) The epidemiology of suicide and suicidal behaviour. In Nock, M., Borges, G. and Ono, Y.(eds.) *Suicide: Global Perspectives From the WHO World Mental Health Surveys*. New York: Cambridge University Press, pp 5–33.

O'Carroll, P., Berman, A., Maris, R., Moscicki, E., Tanney, B. and Silverman, M. (1996) Beyond the tower of babel: A nomenclature for suicidology. *Suicide and Life-Threatening Behavior,* 26(3): 237–252.

O'Connor, R. and Sheehy, N. (2000) *Understanding Suicidal Behaviour.* Oxford: BPS Blackwell.

Opacka-Juffry, J. (2008) The role of serotonin as a neurotransmitter in health and illness. *British Journal of Neuroscience Nursing,* 4: 6.

Qin, P., Agerbo, E. and Mortenson, P. (2003) Suicide risk in relation to socioeconomic, demographic, psychiatric and familial factors: A national register based study of all suicides in Denmark. *American Journal of Psychiatry,* 160: 765–772.

Senker, C. (2013) *Self Harm.* London: Raintree.

Shneidman, E. (1996) *The Suicidal Mind.* Oxford: Oxford University Press.

Shneidman, E. (1999) Suicide as psychache. In Leenaars, A. (ed.) *Lives and Deaths: Selections from the works of Edwin S. Shneidman.* Philadelphia: Taylor & Francis Group, pp 239–244.

Tabachnick, N. and Farberow, N. (1961) The assessment of self-destructive potentiality. In Faberow, N. and Shneidman, E. (eds.) *The Cry for Help.* New York: McGraw Hill Book Company, pp 60–77.

Thomson, A. (2006) *The Making of Social Theory: Order, Reason & Desire.* Oxford: Oxford University Press.

Van Heeringen, C., Portzky, G. and Audenaert, K. (2004) The psychobiology of suicidal behaviour. In DeLeo, D., Bille-Brahe, U., Kerkhof, A. and Schmidtke, A. (eds.) *Suicidal Behaviour; Theories and Research Findings.* Cambridge: Hogrefe and Huber Publishers, pp 61–66.

Varnik, P. (2012) Suicide in the world. *International Journal of Environmental Research and Public Health,* 9: 760–770.

Williams, M. (1997) *Cry of Pain: Understanding Suicide and Self Harm.* London: Penguin Books.

CHAPTER 2

Self-Harm, Suicide and Stigma

Brian Keogh

Introduction

Stigma comprises of three interrelated problems: knowledge (ignorance), attitudes (prejudice) and behaviour (discrimination) (Thornicroft et al., 2007). This chapter will use stigma theory to help readers understand the complexity and impact of stigma on those affected by suicide and self-harm. It will examine ways of addressing stigma towards suicide using macro-interventions such as educational, contact and challenging actions. Furthermore it will provide strategies to assist those affected by stigma to manage issues such as low self-worth, negative self-belief and discrimination. While it is not my intention to associate suicide and self-harm suicidal behaviour to a purely illness interpretation, throughout the chapter, I have often referred to stigma and mental illness to highlight or exemplify different concepts.

LEARNING OUTCOMES

By the end of this chapter, you should be better able to:

1. understand the concept of stigma;
2. describe how suicide and self-harm are stigmatised;
3. understand how stigma is managed at a public policy level;
4. describe strategies that can be used to assist people who are feeling stigmatised because of their experiences of suicide and self-harm.

What is stigma and how does it affect people?

When individuals want to know about stigma they usually go to the work of Erving Goffman who wrote a detailed book in 1963 called *Stigma: Notes on the Management of a Spoiled Identity*. In that book, Goffman describes stigma as attributes that are extremely discrediting for those who possess them. Hinshaw (2007: 23) provides more detail in his definition of stigma:

Stigma refers to a global devaluation of certain individuals on the basis of some characteristic they possess, related to membership in a group that is disfavoured, devalued, or disgraced by the general society. Its connotations imply harsh moral judgements placed on those who are linked to the group in question.

For many people, stigma happens as part of a process. For example, when they come into contact with the mental health services, a number of attitudes and beliefs are applied to them by their peers. These attitudes and beliefs are generally based on stereotypes that society holds about certain individuals, in this case, people with mental health problems. This process, known as labelling, assigns very general characteristics to a large group of heterogeneous individuals. For example, the belief that people who engage in self-harm are 'attention seeking' is a common stereotype. In practice, this is translated to mean that everyone who engages in self-harm is 'attention seeking'. Stereotypes are very much embedded into people's sub-consciousness and are generally not based on individual experience, but rather on the social dialogue that occurs as part of their conversations with their peers or from the media. For that reason they can be difficult to challenge and shift. For many individuals, these stereotypes are also applied to themselves by themselves, resulting in low self-worth and a negative outlook in terms of their ability to challenge the stigma applied to them. To reiterate the example above, the commonly held belief that individuals who engage in self-harm are 'attention seeking' may prevent individuals from seeking help for fear that they will be perceived in this way.

While there is some evidence that the general population have a more positive and enlightened attitude towards people with mental health problems, there is still evidence that stigma continues to exist. For example, a study commissioned by See Change in Ireland (Jupp et al., 2010) suggested that attitudes towards people with mental health problems were positive and demonstrated tolerance. However, a study conducted by Amnesty International in the same year and country catalogued the experiences of stigma for people with mental health problems (64% said that they had been treated unfairly by their friends, 61% reported being treated unfairly by their family and 58% reported being treated unfairly by mental health staff). This demonstrates negative experiences even in a seemingly tolerant society. There are different ways that stigma manifests for affected individuals and their families (Table 2.1):

Table 2.1 Different types of stigma

Types of stigma	Explanation
Felt stigma or self-stigma	This occurs when the affected person applies the negative attitudes and beliefs to themselves. For example, the person feels guilty or ashamed because they engage in self-harm.
Enacted stigma	This occurs when the negative stereotypes, attitudes and beliefs are applied to individuals by their social audience. Enacted stigma exists on a continuum which ranges in intensity. For example, a doctor or nurse who does not believe in a person's potential to recover because they

continued overleaf

Table 2.1   *continued*

Types of stigma	Explanation
	have a mental health problem is a form of enacted stigma. From the earlier example, the belief that all people who engage in deliberate self-harm are 'attention seeking' is also another form of enacted stigma. Not hiring someone for a particular job because they have a mental health problem is enacted stigma as well. So in terms of a continuum, enacted stigma ranges from holding negative attitudes and beliefs to actual discrimination
Courtesy stigma	Courtesy stigma occurs when the family and friends of people who are stigmatised also experience stigma in some shape and form. This may manifest as a negative attitude towards a person's entire family because one person engages in self-harm or individuals being avoided following the death of a family member by suicide.
Structural discrimination	While this is not a type of stigma that affects people at an individual level, it does have a negative impact nonetheless. Structural discrimination refers to inadequacies in the services that are provided for people with mental health services. This is perhaps due to a history of mental health service users not having a voice in terms of speaking out for better services for fear of being stigmatised. While this has improved over the last number of years, there is still evidence that the mental health services continue to be a 'Cinderella' service. For example, in Ireland, only about 6% of entire health spending is devoted to mental health despite the World Health Organisation's estimations that mental health problems will affect about one in four people at some point in their lives. In the United Kingdom, there have also been reports of mental health budget cuts despite substantial rises in referrals to mental health services (http://www.bbc.co.uk/news/health-25331644).

Stigma and suicide

In terms of suicide and self-harm, there are a number of ways that people or their friends or family are affected by stigma.

1. Firstly, the fear of being stigmatised may prevent or deter people from coming forward and looking for help or telling people how they are feeling.
2. According to the Suicide Prevention Australia (2010), stigma may impact negatively on the sense of connectedness that people require for general well-being, thus heightening their risk for suicide and self-harm.
3. Sometimes when people do open up about their feelings to friends and family, they find that they *are* stigmatised. This sometimes leads them to being socially excluded.

4. People who are feeling suicidal or who are engaging in self-harm may feel guilty and ashamed for feeling the way that they do.
5. Feeling like an outsider may also worsen the feelings that the person is already experiencing.
6. The family of people who are bereaved by suicide may also experience stigma. For example, they may find that they are being avoided by friends and neighbours or they may feel that they are unable to openly discuss their feelings due to fears of being stigmatised.

The following fictitious case outlines how a person was affected by stigma after telling her friends about her self-harming behaviour.

CASE SCENARIO 2.1

Lily, who is 16 years old, has been cutting herself on and off for about two years. While the cuts have been superficial, her family are worried that she will do significant harm to herself either purposely or by accident. She has been to counselling and to see a psychiatrist and while these were helpful, Lily is unable to stop cutting her forearms and legs and this tends to worsen when she is under pressure at school or at home. Recently, Lily decided to tell her friends in school about her self-harm despite her mother's suggestion that she should keep it a secret. When she told her friends, they were initially supportive and helpful; however, in the following few weeks she noticed that she was seeing less and less of them. In addition, she has not received as many text messages from them and a few of her less well-known friends have defriended her from Facebook. Last week she discovered that a number of friends were going to a party that she had not been invited to. This made her feel lonely, sad and rejected, and on the night of the party, she inflicted several lacerations to her wrists, forearms and legs. When her mother found her, she was tearful and inconsolable. She was taken to the emergency department by her parents because they didn't know what to say or do.

Why are suicide and self-harm stigmatised?

According to Joiner (2010), there are a multitude of myths and misunderstandings about suicide and self-harm and these impede our ability to fully understand and respond to people who are suicidal or who engage in self-harm. Furthermore, suicide has been stigmatised for hundreds of years again highlighting the difficulties in challenging myths and stereotypes because they are so ingrained into the public consciousness. According to Suicide Prevention Australia (2010), there are a number of reasons why suicide and self-harm remain a stigmatised subject:

- Suicide and religion have had a very close relationship in the past. In many religions including Christianity, Islam and Judaism, suicide was considered a mortal sin and those who died by suicide were seen as going against God's wishes as the creator of life.

- In many countries, suicide was illegal and therefore a crime. People were said to have 'committed' suicide and this language continues to persist in many areas. The decriminalisation of suicide is a relatively modern event (in Ireland it was decriminalised in 1993, in the United Kingdom it was decriminalised in 1961). Prior to this, people who attempted suicide and their families could be prosecuted.
- There are also persistent stereotypes that suicide is a cowardly and selfish act and that people who die by suicide or who engage in self-harm are weak.
- Sometimes it is believed that people who are suicidal are beyond help and if they have made their mind up about taking their own lives, there is nothing that can be done about it.
- Suicide is sometimes seen as a voluntary option where the individual makes a choice and chooses to end their life.
- A lack of understanding about the nature of self-harm may lead people to think that engaging in self-harm is attention seeking, stupid or disgusting.

While some of the myths associated with suicide and self-harm have diminished over time, there is widespread misunderstanding of suicide or the reasons why people engage in self-harm which perpetuates stigma and may prevent affected individuals from seeking help. Furthermore, the family and friends of affected individuals may also experience stigma which may also impact on their grieving process following the death of a loved one by suicide or to support their family member who is engaging in self-harm. There are also myths surrounding interventions and strategies that actually help to reduce the risk of suicide and self-harm. For example, the National Strategy and Action Plan to Prevent Suicide in Scotland (2011) suggests that there is a belief that talking to people about suicide will encourage suicide attempts. They challenge this by arguing that talking to people about their feelings in relation to suicide is helpful and can be a relief to people and can be a key preventative strategy.

Addressing suicide stigma

Thornicroft et al. (2007) suggest that while there is large number of studies that describe people's attitudes to mental illness in general, there is a lack of studies that describe effective interventions. According to a Vision for Change (Department of Health and Children (DOHC), 2006), which outlines current mental health policy in Ireland, mental health stigma reduction comprises three overarching strategies or actions: Educational actions, contact actions and challenging actions. Educational actions aim to provide the general public with information about mental health problems in order to prevent misinterpretations and to demystify and normalise mental distress. Contact actions, on the other hand, work to increase the visibly of people with mental health problems (e.g. through the provision of community-orientated services). Finally, challenging actions aim to challenge the negative stereotypes and beliefs about people with mental health problems through the provision of accurate information about mental illness (DOHC, 2006).

In many countries there are specific organisations which have the remit to tackle the public's perceptions of mental illness and suicide. In Ireland, the organisation is called 'See Change' (www.seechange.ie) and in England it is called 'Time to Change' (www.time-to-change.org.uk). Central to how these organisations work is the creation of an open dialogue and discussion about mental health issues which encourages normalisation and help seeking. For example, the 'Make a ripple' campaign run by See Change in Ireland encouraged the creation of a dialogue about mental health through the use of social media such as Twitter and Facebook. In England, a similar approach called 'Time to talk' is operated and advice on how to start a conversation about mental health is available on their website. For example, the business card (Figure 2.1) encourages individuals to talk to people about mental health and offers advice on how to keep the conversation going. The tagline 'you don't have to be an expert to talk about mental health' promotes the idea that mental health issues affect everyone and that professional help is not the only help that is available.

In relation to suicide and self-harm, The National Strategy and Action Plan to Prevent Suicide in Scotland's 'Choose Life' strategy encourages individuals to talk to people about suicide and suggests that 'if you suspect someone may be feeling suicidal, ask them – it could save their life'. Further examples of how you might invite and encourage someone to talk about their suicidal thoughts and/or behaviours are contained in Chapters 5 and 6.

Health professionals and other agencies

Ucok (2007) suggests that there is some evidence to suggest that a range of mental health professionals can have some negative attitudes towards people with mental health problems. While there is a lack of clarity as to why this occurs, it can impact negatively on service users as health professionals, in

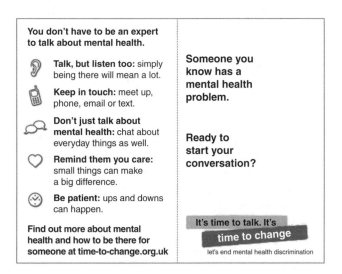

Figure 2.1   'It's time to talk' business card

particular doctors and nurses, are very influential in terms of individuals perceptions of their experiences. In addition, according to Thornicroft (2006), some groups of individuals are more stigmatised that others. For example, those who are diagnosed with borderline personality disorder, who are alcohol dependent and those with an intellectual disability are sometimes viewed in a negative way. In terms of suicide and self-harm, McAllister et al. (2002) found that there was generally a negative attitude towards people who self-harm among emergency department nurses. In a review examining the clinical experiences of people who self-harm (Taylor et al., 2009), the overall experiences reported by the participants were negative with the review citing lack of patient involvement, inappropriate staff behaviour and a lack of knowledge among staff as some of the reasons for this negative experience. Furthermore, the participants suggested that while their physical health was dealt with, their mental health was often ignored (Taylor et al., 2009). A perceived lack of confidence and training in terms of the required interpersonal skills could be one of the reasons that a lack of engagement occurs (Keogh et al., 2007). The emergency department is often the first point of contact for many people who are suicidal or who engage in deliberate self-harm. Within this busy environment, it may also be difficult for staff to find time to engage with individuals who self-harm (Keogh et al., 2007). For health professionals who come into contact with people who self-harm or who are suicidal, some of the strategies that are outlined in the following chapters will be useful. In addition, some of the following strategies could be considered:

- If you are in regular contact with people who engage in self-harm or who are suicidal, you should consider engaging in some specialised education and training. For example, the ASIST (Applied Suicide Intervention Skills Training) programme is a two-day programme open to both professionals and the general public which aims to equip participants with skills to provide emergency first aid mental health to individuals at risk of suicide and suicidal behaviour (Public Health Agency, 2011). More information about the ASIST programme is available at the following website: www.livingworks.net
- The National Strategy and Action Plan to Prevent Suicide in Scotland (2011) suggests that you should ask individuals about their intentions regarding suicide and self-harm in a caring and supportive way. Key to this is giving individuals time to talk, showing them that you care and that you are there to help them. Key strategies that are perceived as helpful by people who engage in self-harm are interpersonal in nature and consist of non-judgemental interactions and active listening (see Chapters 5 and 6 for further information on some of these strategies).
- Be aware of your own values and attitudes about people who are suicidal or who engage in self-harm, try not to let negative experiences that you have had in the past influence how you react.
- Avoid paternalistic, patronising or clichéd responses.
- Encourage the individual to talk about their feelings and be sympathetic to their experiences.

- Openly talking about suicide and self-harm is key to reducing the stigma associated with it.
- Educate yourself about suicide and self-harm.

REFLECTIVE EXERCISE

> Reflecting on your own area of practice/work, which of the above strategies would you feel comfortable using? Which ones do you think are difficult for you? Give reasons for your answer.

Suicide survivors and stigma

The issue of postvention and bereavement following the death of a loved one from suicide is covered in more detail in Chapter 9 of this book (these individuals are known as suicide survivors). There is some debate as to the commonalities and differences between the grief experiences following the death of a loved one from suicide and other sudden deaths. One main difference that has been put forward is that suicide survivors may experience social stigma and this may interfere and disrupt the bereavement process. According to Cvinar (2005: 20), 'stigma remains an integral part of the suicide bereavement process and has a significant influence on psychological wellbeing following the suicide event'. Feigelman et al.'s (2009) study found that their participants experienced real and perceived stigma experiences and that these experiences made the grieving process difficult and in some cases placed the survivors at an increased risk for depression and suicidal thinking. The study further suggested that survivors were stigmatised in the three ways as indicated in Table 2.2 following the death of their child:

Table 2.2   Survivors' experiences of stigma following suicide (Feigelman et al., 2009: 603)

Theme	Explanation
A wall of silence	There was avoidance of any discussion about the death of the child.
The absence of a caring interest	There was limited, if any, discussion about the survivors' well-being.
Unhelpful advice	There was some evidence that others disregarded the impact of the death in terms of the survivors' ability to grieve.

While the experiences documented in Table 2.2 are drawn from one study on survivors' experiences of stigma, they do present some areas that can be considered by individuals who may come into contact with people in distress following the death of a loved one:

1. Talk about the person who died and share memories that you have of them. Use their name when talking about them.
2. Give the survivor time and space to talk about the event. Listen to the person and let them know that you are there for them.
3. Avoid generalising the grieving experience; everyone will grieve differently and in their own time. Avoid giving advice or using clichés.

These and other strategies are discussed in more detail in Chapter 9.

Helping individuals manage stigma

While being stigmatised is difficult for people who engage in suicide and self-harm, they may have a heightened awareness of the fact that they belong to a stigmatised group and internalise that stigmatised identity (felt or self-stigma). This may result in them believing in and accepting the negative beliefs that others hold about them. Angell et al. (2005: 70) have eloquently described self-stigma and its effects in the following quotation:

> That is, consumers develop stereotypic understandings about mental illness through their socialisation and membership in the broader culture, and apply these negative stereotypes to themselves after they are formally labelled. These stereotypes lead consumers to believe that they will be devalued and rejected by others, causing them to withdraw from connections and opportunities, to behave defensively and to experience the loss of self-esteem.

Consequently, there may be worsening of self-harming behaviour, lowered self-esteem and perhaps a reluctance to seek help or disclose any sort of suicidal feelings. While one way of addressing this problem is to reduce the stigma within the general population and to change people's attitudes and perceptions towards suicide and self-harm, this is not easy given the complexities of those beliefs. For people who do internalise these feelings, it is important that they are able to challenge these negative self-perception either within a therapeutic relationship such as in counselling or psychotherapy and/or with education. In addition, they may benefit from support either from their immediate support network or through peer support in the form of peer-led support groups. Furthermore, issues of disclosure (e.g. in work or to friends) may need to be thought about carefully in terms of the advantages and disadvantages about opening up about a history of self-harm and the potential impact that this might have. According to Corrigan & O'Shaughnessy (2007), encouraging people to publically disclose their experiences makes an enormous contribution to reduce stigma. While organisations like *See Change* and *Time to Change* advocate an open dialogue about mental health issues, individuals that do decide to be open about their experiences may receive a negative reaction and should be prepared for this.

The role of the media and suicide and self-harm

According to the media guidelines for reporting suicide and self-harm (The Irish Association of Suicidology & Samaritans, 2013), the media has a responsibility to report suicide and self-harm in a sensitive and non-sensational way. Insensitive and sensationalist reporting of suicide and self-harm has the potential to increase misunderstandings about suicide and self-harm, consequently increasing the stigma that surrounds it. The accurate and sensitive reporting of suicide is discussed in more detail in Chapter 9.

Conclusion

This chapter has introduced the reader to the concept of stigma in relation to suicide and self-harm. While there has been a consistent drive to eradicate the stigma associated with mental health issues generally, both felt and enacted stigma continue to be a problem for people who engage in suicidal behaviour. On a more positive note, Witte et al. (2010) suggest that there is reason for cautious optimism as they found in their study that attitudes towards suicide showed some improvement over time. However, they argue that it is not time for complacency. Ultimately, everyone has a role in reducing the prevalence of stigma towards suicide and self-harm.

REFLECTIVE QUESTIONS

1. Why do you think that suicide and self-harm have been stigmatised throughout history?
2. In terms of stigma prevention and suicide and self-harm, can you think of any contact, educative or challenging actions that have occurred in your community or environment?
3. What do you think the impact of stigma is on people who are suicidal or who engage in self-harm?
4. A friend who has a history of self-harm has a job interview and is anxious to decide if she should tell her prospective employers about it. How might you assist her make the decision to disclose or not?

REFERENCES

Angell, B., Cooke, A. and Kovac, K. (2005) First person accounts of stigma. In Corrigan, P. (ed.) *On the Stigma of Mental Illness: Practical Strategies for Research and Social Change.* Washington DC: American Psychological Association, pp 69–98.

Corrigan, P. and O'Shaughnessy, J. (2007) Changing mental illness stigma as it exists in the real world. *Australian Psychologist,* 42(2): 90–97.

Cvinar, J. (2005) Do suicide survivors suffer social stigma: A review of the literature. *Perspectives in Psychiatric Care,* 41(1): 14 –21.

Department of Health & Children. (2006) *'A Vision for Change' Report of the Expert Group on Mental Health Policy.* Dublin: Stationary Office.

Feigelman, W., Gorman, B. and Jordan, J. (2009) Stigmatisation and suicide bereavement. *Death Studies*, 33: 591–608.

Goffman, E. (1963) *Stigma: Notes on the Management of a Spoiled Identity*. London: Penguin Books.

Hinshaw, S. (2007) *The Mark of Shame: Stigma of Mental Illness and the Agenda for Change*. Oxford: Oxford University Press.

Irish Association of Suiciology & Samaritans. (2013) *Media Guidelines for Reporting Suicide and Self- Harm*. Available from http://www.nosp.ie/media_guidelines.pdf.

Joiner, T. (2010) *Myths About Suicide*. Cambridge: Harvard University Press.

Jupp, R., Burns, V. and Dungan, L. (2010) *Public Attitudes Towards Mental Illness: A Benchmark Study for See Change*. Dublin: Millward Brown. Retrieved from http://www.seechange.ie/index.php/news/68-public-attitudes-towards-mental-health-problems on the 27 November 2013.

Keogh, B., Doyle, L. and Morrissey, J. (2007) Suicidal behaviour. A study of emergency nurses' educational needs when caring for this patient group. *Emergency Nurse*, 15(3): 30–35.

McAllister, M., Creedy, D., Moyle, W. and Farrugia, C. (2002) Nurses attitudes towards clients who self-harm. *Journal of Advanced Nursing*, 40(5): 578–586.

Public Health Agency. (2011) *All Island Evaluation of Applied Suicide Intervention Skills Training (ASIST)*. Dublin: Public Health Agency.

Suicide Prevention Australia. (2010) *Position Statement: Overcoming the Stigma of Suicide*. New South Wales: SPA.

Taylor, T., Hawton, K., Fortune, S. and Kapur, N. (2009) Attitudes towards clinical services among people who self-harm: Systematic review. *The British Journal of Psychiatry*, 194: 104–110.

The National Strategy and Action Plan to Prevent Suicide in Scotland. (2011) *The Art of Conversation: A Guide to Talking, Listening and Reducing Stigma Surrounding Suicide*. Scottish Government.

Thornicroft, G. (2006) *Shunned: Discrimination Against People with Mental Illness*. Oxford: Oxford University Press.

Thornicroft, G., Rose, D., Kassam, A. and Sartorius, N. (2007) Stigma: Ignorance, prejudice or discrimination? *British Journal of Psychiatry*, 190: 192–193.

Ucok, A. (2007) Other people stigmatize ... but, what about us? Attitudes of mental health professionals towards patients with schizophrenia. *Archives of Neuropsychiatry*, 44, 108–116.

Witte, T., Smith, A. and Joiner, T. (2010) Reasons for cautious optimism? Two studies suggesting reduced stigma against suicide. *Journal of Clinical Psychology*, 66(6): 611–626.

CHAPTER 3

Risk and Protective Factors for Self-Harm and Suicide

Louise Doyle

Introduction

Many studies have tried to identify the predictors of self-harm and suicide from various theoretical perspectives, but as seen in Chapter 1, no universal model explains either phenomenon conclusively. The likelihood of a person engaging in self-harm/suicidal behaviour is influenced by a range of psychological, biological, social and environmental risk and protective factors. Identification of factors that may increase or decrease a person's level of risk can contribute towards the assessment of self-harm/suicide risk. Risk and protective factors include those that are modifiable and non-modifiable and they may be distal or proximal. Distal risk factors are those which suggest an underlying vulnerability to self-harm or suicide but do not predict that self-harm or suicide is imminent. Conversely, proximal risk factors are those which represent immediate vulnerability to self-harm or suicide or those which may precipitate a suicidal act. It is important to note that the presence of no one risk factor will determine if a person will become suicidal or engage in self-harm, just as the presence of no one protective factor will guard against suicidal thoughts and behaviours. Rather the development of suicidality and self-harm is the result of a complex interplay of various factors including the presence of some risk factors and the absence of some protective factors. It is important to note that while self-harm and suicide are conceptually different with different functions, intentions and methods, they share a number of similarities in terms of risk and protective factors.

This chapter will present commonly identified risk and protective factors for self-harm and suicidal behaviour and will also identify more specific warning signs of imminent suicidal behaviour. Where differences do exist in terms of risk factors for self-harm and suicide, these will be identified. While some of these factors have been touched on in Chapter 1, they will be described in more detail here. Two case scenarios are presented along with reflective questions which should help the reader to apply the learning in this chapter in real-life scenarios.

LEARNING OUTCOMES

By the end of this chapter, you should be better able to:

1. identify the main risk factors for self-harm and suicide;
2. describe those factors that might protect against self-harm and suicide;
3. outline warning signs for imminent suicidal behaviour;
4. practice asking questions about risk and protective factors concerning self-harm and suicide.

Risk factors for self-harm and suicidal behaviour

In this section, risk factors have been separated into two groups; the first concentrates on psychological/mental health and personal factors while the second focuses on social and environmental factors.

Psychological/mental health and personal factors

A number of psychological/mental health factors, including the mental health history of family members, in addition to personality traits have been linked to self-harm and suicidal behaviour.

Psychological and mental health factors

Risk factors for completed suicide are essentially the characteristics of those individuals who have died by suicide. One of the main methods used to establish these characteristics is through the use of psychological autopsies. As the name suggests, a psychological autopsy involves the meticulous collection of data which helps reconstitute the psychosocial environment of individuals who have died by suicide thereby providing a better understanding of the circumstances of their death (Inserm, 2005). Studies involving psychological autopsy gather information on a large number of areas including details about the person's family background, history of mental health problems, past suicide attempts if any, employment, physical health, stressful life events and social interactions. A psychological autopsy will also determine whether any contact was made with any help/health service prior to the suicide. Most of this information is gathered through interviews with significant others, including the person's family and friends and any health care personnel involved in the person's care. Although psychological autopsies can provide some vital information about a person who has died by suicide, they can also be problematic. The reliance on the interviewing of family and friends to assign a diagnosis posthumously is one area of contention when it comes to psychological autopsies of those who died by suicide. Hjelmeland et al. (2012) have identified that one of the main methodological flaws of psychological autopsy studies is that it is questionable to assign psychiatric diagnoses to someone who is dead by interviewing someone else. When it comes to determining the risk factors for attempted suicide or self-harm, the process becomes a little clearer as the person themselves is the main data source.

Psychological autopsy studies carried out on those who have died by suicide suggest that the majority of those who die by suicide had a mental health problem at the time of their death. One of the first and most widely reported of these psychological autopsies was conducted in Britain by Barraclough et al. (1974) and it demonstrated that in a review of over 100 deaths by suicide, 93% were diagnosed as having a mental illness. Of these, 70% had a depressive illness, while 15% had alcoholism. A more recent systematic review of psychological autopsy studies found that between 90 and 95% of those who died by suicide had a diagnosable mental health problem at the time of their death (Cavanagh et al., 2003). The majority of those had depression, although there were also a significant number who had co-morbidity with another mental health problem or who had co-morbidity with a substance abuse problem. A number of theories exist which seek to explain the link between mental illness and suicidal behaviour (Mishara & Chagnon, 2011). These include:

(i)   that suicidal behaviour and mental illness have common determinants (e.g. negative early life events) rather than a causal link;
(ii) that suicidal behaviour results from the inadequate or inappropriate treatment of mental illness;
(iii) that suicidal behaviour is a consequence of living with mental illness (e.g. social exclusion often associated with long-term mental illness).

However, the most common explanatory theory for the link between suicidal behaviour and mental illness proposes that suicidal behaviour is a direct consequence of mental illness.

The association of depression with suicidal behaviour is perhaps unsurprising. Suicidal behaviour is more likely to occur when depression is accompanied by hopelessness, anxiety and anhedonia (i.e. the inability to experience pleasure). When it comes to the association between suicidal behaviour and substance mis-use, it appears that suicidal behaviour occurs later in the illness progression and is associated with the co-morbid existence of depression in addition to relationship difficulties and social isolation. The apparent link between depression and suicidal behaviour is worrying in the context of the WHO report which predicts that by 2020, depression will be ranked second among the 10 leading causes of global burden of disease (WHO, 2001). This has potential implications for the incidence of suicidal behaviour globally. In addition to depression and substance mis-use, suicidal behaviour has also been associated with other mental health problems including schizophrenia, anxiety disorders and personality disorders.

While Arsenault-Lapierre et al. (2004) also found that a majority of people who died by suicide in their meta-analysis had a diagnosed mental health problem at the time of their death (87.3%), they also found that gender and geographical differences were also evident. There is considerable variability between studies conducted in different parts of the world. The association between mental illness and suicide is more clearly defined in developed countries than in developing ones. This may be explained to some degree by underdeveloped and inaccessible mental health services, which mean that many people are not seen by a psychiatrist and are not therefore diagnosed with a mental illness. However, there is also the likelihood that cultural, social and economic reasons may be more strongly linked to suicide in developing countries (Chechil & Kutcher, 2012). Mental illness is also a specific risk factor for self-harm; however, there is a weaker strength of association between self-harm and a mental health diagnosis than there is between suicide and a mental health diagnosis. (Brausch & Muehlenkamp, 2013).

Notwithstanding the evidence linking suicidal behaviour to mental illness, it is important to remember that the vast majority of people with a mental health problem will not die by suicide and that many of those who die by suicide do not have a mental illness. This therefore strengthens the argument for looking at other factors that can precipitate suicidal behaviour.

History of self-harm or suicide attempt

It has been well-established in numerous studies that a history of self-harm or previous suicide attempt is a significant risk factor for completed suicide. In the case of self-harm this holds true even when the self-harm act is not accompanied by the intent to die. In the case of actual suicide attempt, it is estimated that up to 50% of those who die by suicide have made at least one previous attempt (Chechil & Kutcher, 2012). For those who have attempted suicide in the past, the risk of completed suicide increases if the suicide attempt was recent, if there was regret about surviving the attempt and if the methods used were highly lethal.

Personality type

McLean et al. (2008) identify that certain personality traits appear to be more closely associated with suicidal behaviour. Included in these traits are impulsiveness, aggression, anger, neuroticism, hopelessness, hostility and anxiety. Impulsiveness and aggression have a stronger association for self-harm than for suicide (Klonsky & Olino, 2008), while hopelessness is more common in those who attempt/die by suicide. There is also a correlation between poor problem-solving skills and increased risk of suicidal behaviour. Those who engage in suicidal behaviour are more likely to use emotion-focused coping skills (e.g. avoidance, substance mis-use) to deal with their problems rather than more adaptive, problem-focused coping skills. Again, there are some differences in problem solving when comparing self-harm and suicide, with those who self-harm being able to generate more alternatives when confronted with a problem than those who attempt/die by suicide. However, while those who self-harm have a greater ability to generate a solution, they still have difficulties in choosing a solution to implement (Nock & Mendes, 2008).

Age and gender

Age and gender are two distal risk factors for suicide. As identified in Chapter 4, younger age groups and older age groups are more at risk for suicide. Generally, suicide rates are high in adolescence/young adulthood, they decrease somewhat during middle adulthood before rising again in early old-age and later old-age. Self-harm, however, is more associated with adolescence and young adulthood than the old-age group. There are also established gender differences in suicidal behaviour, particularly in the Western world. Suicide rates are significantly higher in men than in women, and in the United Kingdom and Ireland, this figure is approximately 3:1. A number of reasons have been put forward to explain this, including primarily that men are less likely to seek help than women. It is suggested that the socialisation of men to believe that 'boys don't cry' means that they do not feel comfortable communicating their distress to others. However, Smyth et al. (2003) suggest that it is *because* of this socialisation that they have never learned when or how to communicate distress. In addition, men are less likely to be diagnosed with depression and they are more likely to exhibit impulsive behaviour and to use more lethal means when engaging in a suicidal act. When it comes to the issue of non-fatal self-harm, however, the rates here are higher in women than men. Some possible explanatory reasons for this phenomenon include the use of less lethal means of suicide attempt in women when compared to men. Self-harm in this context also includes non-suicidal self-injury such as cutting. Females are more likely to use this method of self-injury as a coping mechanism to help regulate emotions and deal with difficult experiences.

Family history of mental illness and suicidal behaviour

In addition to a personal history of mental illness or suicidal behaviour, having a biological relative and in particular a parent with a mental health problem also presents an increased risk. It has not been conclusively demonstrated whether this increased risk is due to genetic transmission – nature – or due to the impact of having a parent with significant mental health problems in the family environment – nurture (e.g. increased stress and negative impact on family life). Brent and Mann (2005) identify how adoption studies have demonstrated a genetic link in familial suicide, as there was a six-time higher rate of suicide in the biological relatives of suicide adoptees than the adopted relatives of the suicide adoptees. Similarly, twin studies would also suggest a genetic link as a higher rate of concordance for suicide, and suicidal behaviour was found in monozygotic compared to dizygotic twins (Brent & Mann, 2005). It appears that a genetic predisposition to self-harm and suicidal behaviour can be inherited through a predisposition to psychiatric disorder or a predisposition to self-harming behaviour independent of psychiatric disorder (Brent & Mann, 2005).

However, it appears that the development of suicidal behaviour in a person whose family member also has a history of mental illness is in effect a combination of both nature and nurture involving the interplay of genes and the environment. Exposure to the suicidal behaviour of a family member (or friend) also leads to an increased risk of suicidal behaviour in an individual. This is particularly the case in younger age groups. It appears that a modelling effect may also be involved in adolescents who have family members engaged in self-harm. Rubenstein et al. (1998) suggest that family suicidality increases the risk by providing the teenager with a model for a potentially lethal solution to psychological pain. It may raise the adolescent's awareness of this particular form of coping and may legitimise it as a way of dealing with distress. Similarly, Hawton et al. (2006) suggest that adolescents may feel more comfortable with the idea of suicidal behaviour in times of distress if other family members have previously used self-harm as a response to crises.

Social/environmental factors

A vast array of social and environmental factors has been identified as being linked to self-harm and suicidal behaviour including completed suicide. Some of the most commonly identified include the following.

Ease of access to methods of suicidal behaviour

Ease of access to means of suicidal behaviour is linked to a higher risk of suicide. This is particularly the case for suicidal behaviour which is impulsive. Reducing access to means is one area where there has been significant attention in terms of suicide prevention. This is discussed in more detail in Chapter 8.

Sexual orientation

International literature suggests that lesbian, gay and bisexual people appear to be at a greater risk of mental health problems including suicidal and self-harming behaviour than heterosexual people (Johnson et al., 2007; King & Merchant, 2008). A number of possible explanations for the link between minority sexual orientation and self-harm/suicidal behaviour have been identified. Meyer (2003) proposes the explanatory conceptual framework of 'minority stress' which postulates that stigma, prejudice and discrimination create a hostile and stressful social environment that contributes to mental health problems in LGB people. Minority stress can be related to the process of 'coming out' and publicly declaring oneself to be gay. A gay person who 'comes out' publicly is at risk of fracturing relationships with family and friends thereby decreasing their social support at a time when it is needed most. The concept of 'internalised homophobia' is also associated with minority stress and resultant mental health problems including self-harm/suicidal behaviour in LGB people. This occurs when a gay person directs society's negative views of homosexuality towards themselves resulting in feelings of poor self-regard, self-loathing and worthlessness (Meyer & Dean, 1998; Rivers, 2004), which in turn may lead to self-harm.

History of abuse

Abuse, and particularly sexual abuse in childhood, is significantly related to both suicide and self-harm. Studies by Noll et al. (2003) and Glassman et al. (2007) suggest that this association is particularly strong for females and is also particularly strong for those who engage in non-fatal self-harm. In an attempt to explain this link, both groups of authors suggest that self-harm represents an internalisation of the original trauma of the abuse. Sexual abuse can have an impact on the severity of self-harm, with chronic and repetitive self-harm, in particular, more associated with sexual abuse (Klonsky & Moyer, 2008).

Unemployment

Unemployment is associated with suicidal behaviour, predominately attempted/completed suicide (Wanberg, 2012), and this is particularly true in the context of long-term unemployment (Milner et al., 2013). There are a number of reasons for this, including the decrease in self-esteem and sense of purpose associated with unemployment. In addition, the financial difficulties that can accompany unemployment, particularly long-term unemployment, can cause significant distress and martial/family difficulties. The anticipated loss of the family home and the associated anxiety and loss of ties appears to be a particular stressor associated with unemployment and subsequent financial hardship (Stack & Wasserman, 2007). In turn these stresses can lead to an increase in depression, anxiety, substance mis-use, and ultimately to suicidal behaviour. However, it may also be the case that an existing mental illness leads to the unemployment, and it is the mental illness that is the risk factor for suicidal behaviour. The psychological effects of unemployment appear to have a greater impact on middle-aged people (35–54 years) when compared to younger people. This may be due to the fact that older people usually have greater financial commitments and may suffer a greater loss in status as a result of being unemployed (Corcoran & Arensman, 2010).

Poverty

Poverty and high levels of deprivation have been found to be associated with suicidal behaviour. Persons living in poverty are more likely to be living in deprived areas with less access to health care, social support, education and employment opportunities and with high prevalence of poor general and mental health (Platt, 2011).

Education

Fewer years of education is associated with an increased risk of suicidal behaviour in developed, high-income countries, and this risk increases with age (Nock et al., 2012). It is possible that negative effects of low educational attainment (e.g. financial hardship, unemployment) may explain this to some degree.

Marital status

Having never married is associated with a higher level of suicidal behaviour. However, those who have been previously married and who are now divorced/remarried are at an even higher risk of suicidal behaviour. In both cases of those who never married and those who married but subsequently divorced, the risk of suicidal behaviour increases with age (Nock et al., 2012). Suicidal behaviour is lowest in those who are in their first marriage. Marriage provides interpersonal support that helps buffer against negative outcomes. Loosing this relationship through separation/divorce or death removes that source of support and is in itself a significant source of stress.

Poor emotional/social supports

Linking in with the previous point on marriage is the issue of the absence of emotional and social supports. Living alone, social isolation and the lack of a support system can significantly increase the risk for suicidal behaviour.

Protective factors for self-harm and suicidal behaviour

Protective factors are those which are believed to reduce the risk for suicidal behaviour and increase resilience and the ability to manage life's challenges. Less attention has been paid to researching protective factors when compared to risk factors for suicidal behaviour. This is evidenced by the fact that up to 2008, there were 23 systematic reviews of risk factors and only one systematic review of protective factors for suicidal behaviour (McLean et al., 2008). As a result, the data to support the existence of various protective factors is not very strong (Chechil & Kutcher, 2012). Furthermore, even less attention is paid to identifying protective factors that are specific to self-harm *or* suicide; however, as it does with risk factors, evidence suggests that there are many similarities in protective factors for both self-harm and suicide. Despite the relative paucity of data relating specifically to protective factors, identifying and understanding those factors which might buffer individuals against suicide or self-harm is important and offers significant opportunities for prevention of suicidal behaviour. The following are some commonly identified protective factors.

Emotional and social support

Having emotional and social support where a person receives care, esteem or comfort from another individual, particularly in difficult times, is a protective factor against suicidal behaviour. This emotional support is important across the lifespan, however supportive relationships are particularly significant in adolescence and young adulthood. A recent large-scale survey on the mental health and well-being of young people in Ireland identified that a factor that significantly increased mental well-being was the presence of 'one good adult', that is an adult in whom the young person could confide (Dooley & Fitzgerald, 2011). The presence of 'one good adult' in a young person's life was associated with a range of protective factors including an increased sense of connectedness to family and friends, higher life satisfaction, lower rates of depression, higher self-esteem and better coping ability. Significantly, the absence of 'one good adult' was associated with a higher rate of self-harm and suicidal behaviour (Dooley & Fitzgerald, 2011).

Sense of connection and belonging

Having a sense of belonging and connection to others, for example family, friends or community, is protective against suicidal behaviour (McLaren & Challis, 2009). Sense of belonging is the experience of feeling valued, accepted and integrated within an environment. This sense of belonging can be protective against suicidal thoughts even in the presence of depressive symptoms (McLaren & Challis, 2009).

Problem-solving ability and adaptive coping strategies

Every person experiences problems and distress at some point in their lives. How these problems are navigated and distress managed is a key indicator of future mental health. The use of adaptive coping strategies which involve actively dealing with problems and seeking help if problems cannot be dealt with alone can be protective against suicidal behaviour (McLean et al., 2008).

Self-esteem

Self-esteem is a personal judgement of self-worth, is a basic feature of mental health and is a protective factor that contributes to better health and positive social behaviour (Mann et al., 2004). Self-esteem influences perceptions and coping behaviour and can act as a buffer against the impact of negative influences (Mann et al., 2004).

Religious beliefs and participation

Belief in a God and participation in religion appear to be protective factors in relation to suicidal behaviour, particularly serious suicide attempts and completed suicide. There are a number of factors which may explain the relationship between low suicide rates and religious beliefs including (i) the sense of belonging and support that comes from being involved in religious networks, (ii) commitment to core religious beliefs and (iii) the existence of religious-based moral sanctions on suicidal behaviour (McLean et al., 2008; Nelson et al., 2012).

CASE SCENARIO 3.1

Risk and protective factors for suicide

Ellen is a 49-year-old, divorced woman who lives with her two teenage children, Emma and James. She works as a solicitor in a reputable but demanding law firm. In recent months, there has been many meetings concerning cost-cutting strategies and the possibility of redundancy or reduction in staff's working hours. Since her recent divorce, Ellen has found it hard to manage financially and is particularly anxious about losing her job. Ellen has noticed that she has become increasingly anxious and finds it difficult to motivate herself; she has experienced fleeting thoughts about taking an overdose and being able to forget about all her worries. Ellen is close to her parents and sister although they live many miles away. She has a few close friends, whom she sees quite regularly. One day, she says jokingly to Hannah her best friend, 'the children would be much better without me – I have a very good insurance policy'.

- What would you say to Ellen?
- What factors and why do you consider put Ellen at risk for a suicide attempt?
- What questions might you ask to elicit further information in order to assess Ellen's potential risk for suicidal behaviour?
- What factors do you consider to be potential protective factors?

CASE SCENARIO 3.2

Risk and protective factors for self-harm

Jack is a 20-year-old college student who lives at home with both his parents. His parents do not have an amicable relationship, and Jack's relationship with them is also strained and not a close one although he is close to his older brother, whom he sees every week. Jack was performing very well academically and was working towards his end of year exams when his girlfriend of two years broke up with him without an indication of there being any difficulties. Jack was very hurt by this and found it very hard to control his emotions. He began to drink alcohol excessively and one evening after drinking at home in his room he cut his forearm with a blade when his girlfriend did not answer his call. This made him feel calmer, and as the damage caused to his arm was relatively superficial, he did not go to hospital for treatment nor did he tell anyone about this incident.

- What would you say to Jack if he did confide in you about his self-harm?
- What factors do you think put Jack at risk of self-harm?
- What factors do you consider to be potential protective factors?
- What factors might put Jack at increased risk for repeated self-harm?

Warning signs of imminent suicidal behaviour

Warning signs for suicide have been defined as 'the earliest detectable sign that indicates heightened risk for suicide in the near term (i.e. within minutes, hours or days)' (Rudd et al., 2006: 258). Warning signs for suicide are present in many cases; however, they are not always obvious. In many cases, warning signs are only observed in retrospect and in some cases no signs of suicidal thought or planning are evident at all. Warning signs and risk factors for suicidal behaviour can overlap, and many warning signs are indeed risk factors for suicidal behaviour. However, warning signs indicate that there is a heightened suicide risk in the short-term and so in that way differ from some more distal suicide risk factors. Additionally warning signs are often more specific than many risk factors which tend to be generic in nature, for example gender, age.

The use of warning signs to alert members of the general public to signs of impending problems is not a new concept; they have been previously used to warn about heart attack and stroke. Similar to these campaigns, warning signs for suicidal behaviour need to be easily understood by the layman. The American Association of Suicidology (AAS) developed a two-tiered set of warning signs for imminent suicidal behaviour identifying what members of the public should do if someone manifests signs of suicidal behaviour (Rudd et al., 2006). These are presented in Box 3.1

BOX 3.1 AAS WARNING SIGNS FOR SUICIDALITY

In this hierarchical list, the individual is directed to **call the emergency services** if:

- **Someone is threatening to hurt or kill themselves**. A direct threat of suicide should always be taken seriously.
- **Someone is looking for ways to kill themselves. Seeking access to pills, weapons or other means.** Having access to means is linked with suicide and particularly impulsive suicide.
- **Someone is talking or writing about death, dying or suicide.** These may be subtle or vague statements or they could be direct statements of intent.

The individual is advised to **contact a mental health professional for advice** should they witness, hear, or see anyone exhibiting any one or more of these behaviours:

- **Hopelessness.** Feeling hopeless about the future with little sense that anything will change.
- **Rage, anger, seeking revenge.** Express or act in ways that express hostility, bitterness, resentment or rage.
- **Acting reckless or engaging in risky activities, seemingly without thinking.** Acting in ways that could be dangerous without caring about the consequences.
- **Feeling trapped – like there's no way out.** They can't see their situation in life improving and cannot see a way out.
- **Increasing alcohol or drug use.** Increasing use of alcohol and/or drugs.
- **Withdrawing from friends, family or society.** They stop engaging with family and friends and doing things they used to do. They become isolated.
- **Anxiety, agitation, unable to sleep or sleeping all the time.** They may appear worried or shaken. They sleep excessively or very little.
- **Dramatic changes in mood.** A dramatic improvement in mood may indicate a decision to die by suicide has been made.
- **No reason for living; no sense of purpose in life.** Life seems pointless.

Conclusion

It is clear from this chapter that suicidal behaviour is a complex phenomenon which is a result of an interplay of factors rather than the presence of one risk factor or the absence of one protective factor. Awareness of some of the factors that can contribute to or protect against suicide and self-harm is important in terms of understanding why people engage in suicidal behaviour. It can also help health professionals establish a level of risk for a person. However, it is imperative to remember that suicide is not always predictable and the presence or absence of risk and protective factors is only one element of a broader picture in suicide risk assessment. Notwithstanding this, evidence-based knowledge about risk and protective factors is important in helping to develop suicide and self-harm prevention initiatives that are tailored to those most at risk.

REFLECTIVE QUESTIONS

1. Think back to someone you worked with who exhibited suicidal behaviour (including self-harm). Can you identify if there were obvious risk factors present – what were they?
2. Identify the warning signs for suicidal behaviour.
3. What action would you take if someone in your personal or professional life exhibited warning signs of suicidal behaviour?
4. Give an example of when a protective factor(s) might change and no longer serve as a specific protective factor for the person?

REFERENCES

Arsenault-Lapierre, G., Kim, C. and Turecki, G. (2004) Psychiatric diagnoses in 3275 suicides: A meta-analysis. *BMC Psychiatry*, 4: 37.

Barraclough, B., Bunch, J., Nelson, B. and Sainsbury, P. (1974) A hundred cases of suicide: Clinical aspects. *British Journal of Psychiatry*, 125: 355–373.

Brausch, A.M. and Muehlenkamp, J. (2013) Self-harm and suicide. In Lester, D. and Rogers, J.R. (eds.) *Suicide: A Global Issue*. California: Greenwood Publishing Group. pp 161–186.

Brent, D.A. and Mann, J.J. (2005) Family genetic studies, suicide, and suicidal behaviour. *American Journal of Medical Genetics*, 133C: 13–24.

Cavanagh, J.T.O., Carson, A.J., Sharpe, M. and Lawrie, S.M. (2003) Psychological autopsy studies of suicide: A systematic review. *Psychological Medicine*, 33(3): 395–405.

Chechil, S. and Kutcher, S. (2012) *Suicide Risk Management: A Manual for Health Professionals*. 2nd ed. Wiley-Blackwell: West Sussex.

Corcoran, P. and Arensman, E. (2010) Suicide and employment status during Ireland's Celtic Tiger economy. *European Journal of Public Health*, 21(2): 209–214.

Dooley, B. and Fitzgerald, A. (2011) *My World Survey: National Study of Youth Mental Health in Ireland*. Headstrong: Dublin.

Glassman, L.H., Weierich, M.R., Hooley, J.M., Deliberto, T.L. and Nock, M.K. (2007) Child maltreatment, non-suicidal self-injury, and the mediating role of self-criticism. *Behaviour Research and Therapy*, 45(10): 2483–2490.

Hawton, K., Rodham, K. and Evans, E. (2006) *By Their Own Young Hand. Deliberate Self-Harm and Suicidal Ideas in Adolescents*. London: Jessica Kingsley Publishers.

Hjelmeland, H.M., Dieserud, G., Dyregrov, K., Knizek, B.L. and Leenaars, A.A. (2012) Psychological autopsy studies as diagnostic tools: Are they methodologically flawed? *Death Studies*, 36(7): 605–626.

Inserm. (Institut national de la santé et de la recherche médicale) (2005) *Suicide: Psychological Autopsy, a Research Tool for Prevention*. Paris: Inserm Collective Expertise Group. Available from: http://www.ncbi.nlm.nih.gov/books/NBK7126/

Johnson, K., Faulkner, P., Jones, H. and Welsh, E. (2007) *Understanding Suicidal Distress and Promoting Survival in Lesbian, Gay, Bisexual and Transgender (LGBT) Communities*. Brighton & Hove: HSRPC.

Klonsky, E.D. and Moyer, A. (2008) Childhood sexual abuse and non-suicidal self-injury: Meta analysis. *British Journal of Psychiatry*, 192(3): 166–170.

Klonsky, E.D. and Olino, T.M. (2008) Identifying clinically distinct subgroups of self-injurers among young adults: A latent class analysis. *Journal of Consulting and Clinical Psychology*, 76(1): 22–27.

King, C.A. and Merchant, C.R. (2008) Social and interpersonal factors relating to adolescent suicidality: A review of the literature. *Archives of Suicide Research*, 12: 181–196.

Mann, M., Hosman, C.M.H., Schlaalma, H.P. and de Vries, W.K. (2004) Self-esteem in a broad spectrum approach for mental health promotion. *Health Education Research*, 19(4): 357–372.

McLaren, S. and Challis, C. (2009) Resilience among men farmers: The protective role of social support and sense of belonging in the depression-suicidal ideation relation. *Death Studies*, 33(3): 262–276.

McLean, J., Maxwell, M., Platt, S., Harris, F. and Jepson, R. (2008) *Risk and Protective Factors for Suicide and Suicidal Behaviour: A Literature Review*. Edinburgh: Scottish Government Social Research.

Meyer, I. and Dean, L. (1998) Internalised homophobia, intimacy and sexual behaviour among gay and bisexual men. In Herek, G. (ed.) *Stigma and Sexual Orientation*. Thousand Oaks, CA: Sage.

Meyer, I.H. (2003) Prejudice, social stress, and mental health in lesbian, gay and bisexual populations: Conceptual issues and research evidence. *Psychological Bulletin*, 129(5): 674–697.

Milner A., Page, A. and LaMontagne, A.D. (2013) Long-term unemployment and suicide: A systematic review and meta-analysis. *PLoS ONE* 8(1): e51333. doi: 10.1371/journal.pone.0051333

Mishara, B.L. and Chagnon, F. (2011) Understanding the relationship between mental illness and suicide and the implications for suicide prevention. In O'Connor, R.C., Platt, S. and Gordon, J. (eds.) *International Handbook of Suicide Prevention. Research, Policy and Practice*. West Sussex: Wiley-Blackwell.

Nelson, G., Hanna, R., Houri, A. and Klimes-Dougan, B. (2012) Protective functions of religious traditions for suicide risk. *Suicidology Online*, 3: 59–74.

Nock, M.K. and Mendes, W.B. (2008) Physiological arousal, distress tolerance, and social problem-solving deficits among adolescent self-injurers. *Journal of Consulting and Clinical Psychology*, 76(1): 28–38.

Nock, M.K., Deming, C.A., Cha, C.B., Chin, W.T., Hwang, I., Sampson, N.A., Hinkov, H., Lepine, J-P., Ono, Y. and Beautrais, A. (2012) Sociodemographic risk factors for suicidal behaviour: Results from the WHO world mental health surveys. In Nock, M.K., Borges, G. and Ono, Y. (eds.) *Suicide: Global Perspectives from the WHO World Mental Health Surveys*. Cambridge: Cambridge University Press.

Noll, J.G., Horowitz, L.A., Bonanno, G.A., Trickett, P.K. and Putnam, F.W. (2003) Revictimization and self-harm in females who experienced childhood sexual abuse. *Results from a Prospective Study*, 18(12): 1452–1471.

Platt, S. (2011) Inequalities and suicidal behaviour. In O'Connor, R.C., Platt, S. and Gordon, J. (eds.) *International Handbook of Suicide Prevention. Research, Policy and Practice*. West Sussex: Wiley-Blackwell.

Rivers, I. (2004) Recollections of bullying at school and their long-term implications for lesbians, gay men, and bisexuals. *Crisis*, 25(4): 169–175.

Rubenstein, J.L., Halton, A., Kastan, L., Rubin, C. and Stechler, G. (1998) Suicidal behavior in adolescents: Stress and protection in different family contexts. *American Journal of Orthopsychiatry*, 68(2): 274–284.

Rudd, M.D., Berman, A.L., Joiner, T.E., Nock, M.K., Silverman, M.M., Mandrusiak, M., Van Orden, K. and Witte, T. (2006) Warning signs for suicide: Theory, research, and clinical applications. *Suicide and Life-Threatening Behavior*, 36(3): 255–262.

Smyth, C., MacLachlan, M. and Clare, A. (2003) *Cultivating Suicide? Destruction of Self in a Changing Ireland*. Dublin: Liffey Press.

Stack, S. and Wasserman, I. (2007) Economic strain and suicide risk: A qualitative analysis. *Suicide and Life-Threatening Behavior*, 37(1): 103–112.

Wanberg, C.R. (2012) The individual experience of unemployment. *The Annual Review of Psychology*, 63: 369–396.

World Health Organisation. (2001) *Mental Health: A Call for Action by World Health Ministers*. Geneva: World Health Organisation.

CHAPTER 4

Suicide and Self-Harm Across the Lifespan

Louise Doyle

Introduction

Patterns of self-harm and suicide differ across the lifespan with suicide peaking in adolescence/early adulthood and again in old age, while self-harm is predominately a feature of adolescence and early adulthood. The previous chapter has identified the risk and protective factors for self-harm and suicide; however, the factors affecting a person's decision to harm themselves or deliberately end their life can change as they move from childhood through adolescence, adulthood and on to old age. This chapter will look at each stage of life and will discuss the specific issues that influence patterns of self-harm and suicide in childhood, adolescence, adulthood and old age. The emphasis in this chapter will be on recognising age-specific factors which influence self-harm and suicidal behaviour. There is a particular focus on adolescence and old age as there are more age-specific risk factors relating to these two transitional life stages in comparison to middle-age. As suicidal behaviour in children is relatively rare, it is only covered in brief.

LEARNING OUTCOMES

By the end of this chapter, you should be better able to:

1. identify the different trends in self-harm and suicidal behaviour across the lifespan;
2. describe the main age-specific risk factors for self-harm and suicide in the four life stages;
3. identify how age-related life events can precipitate self-harm and suicide;
4. utilise knowledge of age-specific risk factors in your area of work.

Self-harm and suicide in children

Completed suicide is relatively rare in those up to 15 years of age although prevalence is underestimated due to the reluctance of coroners to assign this verdict (Hawton & James, 2005). Rates of completed suicide in pre-pubertal children are the lowest of all age groups with a global incidence of 0.4 per 100,000 under the age of 15, although the rate has more than doubled since 1960 (Australian Institute for Suicide Research and Prevention, 2003). Many authors when writing about the phenomenon of self-harm and suicide in children (those aged up to 14 years) inextricably link them with adolescents (those aged 14–18 years) and discuss them as one homogenous group. However, there is evidence to suggest that while there are overlapping similarities in the characteristics of self-harm and suicide between children and adolescents, there are also many differences.

Although children who die by suicide have many similarities to older adolescents, Freuchen et al. (2012) found that there was less of a gender difference in those in the younger age group. In addition, there were fewer obvious risk factors and less suicide intent and warning signs than often found with older adolescents. Furthermore, the motivation and meaning ascribed to the suicidal act is often different from that in adolescent and adult suicides (Smyth, MacLachlan & Clare, 2003). A number of studies have identified that most young children hold an immature view of death which may in turn contribute to facilitating suicidal behaviour in this cohort. Part of this immature view includes the belief that death is not permanent but is a temporary pleasant state which will relieve all tensions and anxieties. This would suggest that in helping potentially suicidal children, their understanding of suicide and what happens when they die needs to be taken into account (Mishara, 1999). Suicidal behaviour in children is more impulsive than in any other age group. They are more likely to engage in an impetuous self-destructive act such as jumping from a high place or running in front of a car. They are less likely to engage in suicidal behaviour that involves planning such as hoarding drugs with a view to overdose. Intent is further questioned when considering the most common method of completed suicide in children, which is hanging/strangulation (Hepp et al., 2012), as there is debate regarding whether some of these deaths are actually the unintended consequences of what is commonly referred to as the 'choking game'; an asphysixal game in which pressure is applied to the neck to produce a feeling of euphoria (Macnab et al., 2009).

Although there are fewer obvious risk factors for suicidal behaviour in childhood, there are still some relevant factors to be aware of including:

- Previous history of suicide attempt
- Presence of mental health problems
- Preoccupation with death
- Family history of suicide or mental health difficulties
- Negative home environment
- Physical and/or sexual abuse
- Loss of emotionally important people through death/separation. (Tishler et al., 2007)

Self-harm and suicide in adolescents

While suicidal behaviour is rare in children, it becomes increasingly frequent with age, hence adolescents are one of the main targets of suicide prevention initiatives. Adolescence is a period of transition, a time when young people experience a range of emotional, physical and social changes. As a life stage it can be a difficult time, as young people grapple with these changes and increased societal pressures. While most adolescents will navigate successfully through this period experiencing only 'normal emotional turmoil' (Freake et al., 2007), a significant minority will develop more serious emotional and mental health problems. The impact of even a relatively mild mental health problem in adolescence can have a profound effect on later adult life with substantial disruptive effects on social relationships, quality of life and the establishment of adult roles (Chen et al., 2006). Many mental health problems emerge during adolescence and early adulthood. In particular, self-harm and suicidal behaviour usually emerges during adolescence and increases during later adolescence and is considered to be one of the most important social and healthcare problems for this cohort (Hawton et al., 2006).

Self-harm peaks in adolescence, and while suicide is uncommon in adolescence compared with non-fatal self-harm, there is a considerable link between the two with prospective studies showing a substantial risk of suicide after hospital-treated adolescent self-harm (Hawton et al., 2012). Findings which report on the prevalence of self-harm in adolescence suggest that it is a global public health problem with community studies identifying that approximately 10% of adolescents engage in self-harm (Hawton et al., 2012). In Ireland, the only country to have a national register reliably identifying all presentations to hospital for self-harm, figures have shown that highest rates of self-harm are consistently among young people and in particular in girls aged 15–19 years (Griffin et al., 2014). Hospital-treated self-harm is also common in England and Wales where there are approximately 142,000 presentations annually to hospital for assessment and treatment of self-harm; 25,000 of which are young people (Hawton et al., 2000). While self-harm represents one of the most common reasons for hospital presentation by adolescents, it is recognised that hospital-based figures significantly under-represent the true extent of self-harm as most of those who self-harm do not go to hospital for treatment and are therefore not represented in official statistics. Variations in reporting of completed suicide make it difficult to compare rates across different countries; however, overall suicide is the second most common cause of death in adolescents globally after road traffic accidents, with adolescent males 2.6 times more likely to die by suicide than females (Hawton et al., 2012).

As with any age group, the motivation behind self-harm and suicidal behaviour in adolescence is complex. A number of studies report that when presented with a list of potential motives for self-harm, the most frequently reported motives are the desire to escape from a terrible state of mind and wanting to die (Hawton et al., 2002; Scoliers et al., 2009). Two important points should be noted here: (1) In most cases, those who reported wanting to die as a motive for their self-harm also reported an additional motive suggesting some ambivalence about death and (2) Commonly ascribed motivations such as 'seeking attention' or 'wanting to frighten someone' are not commonly reported by adolescents who self-harm, suggesting that these motives are more frequently attributed to these adolescents by others (Scoliers et al., 2009).

As identified in the previous chapter, there are a number of factors associated with adolescent self-harm and suicide that are common across all age groups including depression, anxiety, substance misuse, low self-esteem and a history of sexual abuse. However, the adolescent period brings with it a number of challenges that are unique to this age group and contribute to the risk of self-harm and suicide in those with few protective factors. Although there are some differences in epidemiology and significant differences in function between suicide and non-fatal self-harm, most of the common characteristics of adolescents who self-harm are similar to those who die by suicide (Hawton et al., 2012). The following are some of the factors that have been identified in international studies as being associated with adolescent suicidal behaviour including self-harm:

- *Parental–family conflicts*: A number of family factors have been associated with self-harm and suicide in adolescents including parental criticism and alienation and a poor-quality parent–adolescent relationship (Hilt et al., 2008; Hawton et al., 2012).
- *Family structure*: A non-intact family structure and parental divorce have been associated with self-harm and suicidal behaviour (Tobias et al., 2010). However, there are some equivocal findings with some studies finding that a good parent–adolescent relationship provided protection against self-harm and suicide in non-intact family structures (Flouri & Buchanan, 2002).
- *Bullying*: An association has been reported between bullying and adolescent self-harm and suicide. While bullying occurs in all schools and is a relatively common experience, it can be a significant source of stress for young people. The experience of isolation as a result of victimisation and the absence of protective peer factors (Meland et al., 2010) appear to contribute to the higher incidence of self-harm and suicidal behaviour in adolescents who are bullied.
- *Sexual orientation*: Young people who are gay, lesbian and bisexual appear to be at greater risk of mental health problems including self-harm and completed suicide (Portzky et al., 2008). Issues including minority stress, internalised homophobia and homophobic bullying (Mayock et al., 2008) have been identified as possible contributory factors to the relatively high levels of self-harm and suicidal behaviour in gay, lesbian and bisexual young people.
- *Problems with school work*: Poor school performance or problems at school are reported to have an association with self-harm and suicidal behaviour in a number of studies. However, it is unclear whether having difficulties at school contributes to suicidal behaviour or whether those who engage in suicidal behaviour disengage from school and the academic process in general (Hawton et al., 2006).
- *Impulsivity*: Although impulsivity is a risk factor across the lifespan, it has particular relevance to the adolescent cohort with a large number of studies finding a relationship between adolescent self-harm and impulsivity. Indeed, Hawton et al. (1982), reporting on adolescents who had presented to emergency departments following self-poisoning, found that half of the

50 adolescents had thought about it for less than 15 minutes, while only four thought about it for more than 24 hours. As identified in the previous chapter, although impulsivity is a risk factor for both self-harm and suicide, it appears to have a stronger association for self-harm than suicide (Klonsky & Olino, 2008).

- *Exposure to self-harm and suicidal behaviour of a friend*: Adolescent self-harm and suicidal behaviour appears to be significantly associated with knowing a friend who has engaged in suicidal behaviour (Cleas et al., 2010). In an attempt to explain the association between adolescent self-harm and exposure to self-harm in peers, two hypotheses have been proposed. The first centres on 'selection effect', which suggests that adolescents with low self-esteem and vulnerability to self-harm are more likely to associate with similar adolescents. The second hypothesis focuses on a 'contagion effect', which suggests that adolescents engage in self-harm as a result of social learning from peers who also self-harm. Studies which attempt to differentiate selection effects from contagion effects are rare; however, there is evidence to suggest that both mechanisms may be relevant to understanding adolescent self-harm (Joiner, 2003).
- *Exposure to self-harm and suicidal behaviour of a family member*: An association has also been found between exposure to self-harm and suicidal behaviour of a family member and adolescent self-harm (McMahon et al., 2010). It appears that a modelling effect may also be involved in adolescents who have family members who engaged in self-harm. Adolescents may feel more comfortable with the use of self-harm in times of distress if other family members have previously used self-harm as a response to crises (Hawton et al., 2006). Genetics may also have a role to play for the higher rate of suicidal behaviour within families, although familial transmission of suicidal behaviour seems to be independent of the presence of mental illness (Hawton et al., 2012).
- *Problems with friends*: Social isolation from peers and difficulties with peers have been associated with adolescent self-harm and suicidal behaviour.

Regardless of the factors contributing to self-harm and suicidal behaviour, the act of harming oneself is an indication that a young person is in significant psychological distress. Promisingly, recent research reports that most adolescent self-harming resolves spontaneously (Moran et al., 2012) suggesting that self-harm in adolescents may represent a transient period of distress without further risk. However, self-harm and in particular repeated self-harm can be an important indicator of mental health problems, including completed suicide, in later life (Portzky & van Heeringen, 2007). For this reason, assessment of the adolescent following an episode of self-harm is recommended. Adolescents who self-harm are not a homogenous group and therefore require different degrees of support and intervention following the self-harm. A number of treatment options are available and have been utilised by adolescents including cognitive-behavioural therapy, dialectical behavioural therapy, problem-solving and family therapy. However, recent systematic reviews of interventions for adolescents who engage in self-harm concluded that there was insufficient evidence for the effectiveness of interventions for self-harm and suicide among adolescents and identified the need for further research in this area (Ougrin & Latif, 2011).

Self-harm and suicide in early and middle adulthood

In most Western countries, rates of completed suicide peak in early to mid-adulthood. Self-harm in this age group decreases significantly from adolescence. For the purpose of this chapter, early adulthood is considered to include years 25–34, while middle adulthood spans from age 35–64. Although this age group does not have the same extent of physical, psychological and social changes that are present in adolescence and old age, there are still a number of age-related factors that contribute to suicidal behaviour and in particular attempted and completed suicide in this age group. A review of international literature identifies the following age-specific risk factors for suicidal behaviour in adulthood:

- *Unemployment*: Unemployment and, in particular, long-term unemployment is significantly associated with suicidal behaviour. This is especially true for men.
- *Occupational stress*: Being in employment can also cause particular stressors. Completed suicides are known to be higher in certain occupations which can be seen as particularly stressful (e.g. doctors, farmers).
- *Age 30 transition*: An evaluation of previous life decisions often occurs around the age of 30 and has been coined as the 'age 30 transition'. At this time, decisions regarding career, partner, parenting and lifestyle are often evaluated (Stillion & McDowell, 1996). For some, this can be a difficult period and this review of important life decisions may increase suicide risk.
- *Parenthood (including fertility issues)*: Starting a family or trying to start a family can be a stressful time for people. The increasing age of first-time mothers has led to an increase in infertility problems among couples. The stress associated with infertility, and in particular with infertility following treatment, has been linked to an increase in suicide risk in women (Kjaer et al., 2011). However, further research is required in this area.
- *Menopause*: The menopause is a time of significant hormonal change for women. Resulting from the menopause, a number of changes occur. Women lose the ability to become pregnant and may develop an array of physical symptoms ranging from mild and uncomfortable to significantly distressing. Although hormone replacement therapy (HRT) has brought some relief for many women experiencing the menopause, this too is associated with a number of problems. Studies have identified a higher rate of suicide in women currently experiencing the menopause when compared to women before and after menopause and men (Usall et al., 2009); however, this is an area that warrants further research.

The factors identified above have all been linked with suicidal behaviour in early and middle adulthood. However, research about age-specific risk factors in this group is lacking as there is a greater focus on those two age groups with the greatest amount of transition – adolescence and old age. A greater focus on identifying the specific stressors associated with both early and middle adulthood is required.

Self-harm and suicide in the older person

Despite increasing and appropriate attention on the escalating suicide rate in young people over the past two decades, globally suicide rates among older adults are higher than in any other age group. The true incidence may not be accurately identified by official statistics and there is likely to be an under-reporting of death in this group, as it can be difficult for coroners to return a verdict of suicide, as the cause of death may be difficult to determine absolutely. Due to the increasing proportion of older people, the absolute numbers of suicide in this population is expected to increase significantly in the coming decades.

The high suicide rate in the older person may be explained by a number of reasons. It appears that older people have greater suicide intent than younger individuals whose intent to die may be more ambivalent. In addition, it is clear that older people use more lethal means than young people do (Conwell & Thompson, 2008). Physiological changes associated with aging and the increasing possibility of a physical health problem and a greater tendency towards frailty increase the likelihood that a suicide attempt will result in death than would be the case for a fit, young person. Furthermore, older people are more likely to live alone and therefore less likely to be discovered early and rescued following a suicide attempt. They also appear to demonstrate greater planning and engage in suicidal behaviour that is less impulsive than young people. These reasons may contribute to an explanation of not only the high completed suicide rate in this age group but also the lower rate of non-fatal self-harm as it can be suggested that older people who attempt suicide are more likely to die.

Although the suicide rate in older people is high, it is generally decreasing; partly it would seem to be due to increased attention and investment in old-age socio-economic policies including comprehensive retirement cover and post-retirement plans, but it is also due to improvements in treatments for physical and mental health problems in older people. It is important to note, however, that this overall decline in older person suicide is not replicated throughout the world with little decline seen in some Latin countries that appear to have been adversely affected by changes in social structure including changes in family composition from extended families with three generations to extended nuclear families (De Leo & Arnautovska, 2011).

While rates of completed suicide peak in the old-age group, rates of non-fatal self-harm decrease significantly in the older person. While a past history of self-harm is a strong predictor of completed suicide across the lifespan, this is particularly the case for older people. Self-harm becomes more akin to suicide in the old-age group. There is evidence of high suicidal intent in approximately two-thirds of those which is a considerably greater proportion than found amongst younger people (Hawton & Harris, 2006). The gender ratio also resembles that for completed suicide with more males engaging in self-harm in this age group than women (Hawton & Harris, 2008). However, it is important to note that despite the apparent increased seriousness of self-harm in older people; approximately 75% of older adults who die by suicide have never made a prior attempt (Conwell & Thompson, 2008). The vast majority of research conducted in the area of older adult self-harm and suicidal behaviour focuses on attempted and completed suicide. Therefore, the following section details the age-specific risk factors for attempted and completed suicide in older adults.

As with other age groups, mental health problems including depression and anxiety are strongly linked with completed suicide in the older person. Psychological autopsy studies found that the majority of older people who died by suicide were diagnosed with a mental health problem, most often depression (Conwell & Thompson, 2008). However, just as in adolescence, old age is characterised by a series of physical, psychological and social changes, some of which contribute in a unique way to the decision of an older person to take their own life. Some age-specific risk factors for suicidal behaviour in the older person include the following:

- *Physical illness*: The presence of physical illness significantly increases suicide risk across the whole lifespan. The base rate of physical illness, including chronic and physical illness and organic brain conditions such as Alzheimer's disease, is much higher in the older population although the evidence to support a causal link is equivocal (Conwell & Duberstein, 2005). However, it appears that the existence of multiple physical health problems or co-morbidity of physical illness with mental health problems such as depression seems to be a particular cause of an increased suicide risk in older people (De Leo & Arnautovska, 2011). Physical decline may also cause withdrawal from social contact thereby heightening the suicide risk in this group (Stillion & McDowell, 1996). Older people are acutely aware of increasing physical frailty and increasing helplessness and dependency on others which is compounded by a contemporary society which makes repeated reference to the 'burden' of the elderly.
- *More accepting of death*: Society accepts that death in old age is inevitable. Death in younger people is viewed as tragic and untimely while death in older people has a sense of normality about it – this is the way it 'should be'. For this reason many older people are more accepting of death as a concept believing that they have lived a full life and that their time has come.
- *Social isolation and lack of social interaction*: Older people experience increased isolation and loneliness compared to young populations. Adult children have left home, spouses and friends die, and physical ill-health may mean limited opportunity for engagement with others. Although being isolated and lacking social interaction is a risk factor for suicidal behaviour across the lifespan, the life circumstances of older people mean that it is they who are more likely to experience this isolation.

- *Retirement and feelings of loss*: Retirement can be an exceptionally stressful time for many older people. Although there is evidence to suggest that for many retirement is associated with an improvement in mental health, it seems that for some the enthusiasm and excitement of retirement fades particularly from the second year onwards when feelings of boredom and loss intensify. In particular, early retirement appears to have a negative effect on well-being (Butterworth et al., 2006). Loss of driving licence and loss of important body functions such as sight and mobility can also add to the stress burden in old age (Erlangsen et al., 2011).
- *Bereavement*: Older people experience more bereavement than any other age group. The loss of a spouse, friends and family members causes a great deal of distress. The loss of a long-term spouse and constant companion in particular is especially stressful and distressing. Unlike in younger people, these bereavements often occur in rapid succession and this, in addition to the losses stated previously, results in a pattern of cumulative loss which does not allow sufficient time for resolution of the grief before another loss occurs (Stillion & McDowell, 1996).

It has been identified that older people are more likely to see their doctor in the days and weeks preceding a suicidal act (De Leo & Arnautovska, 2011) with as many as three in four older people contacting their doctor one month prior to engaging in suicidal behaviour (Montano, 1999). However, it also appears that many GPs do not identify the mental health difficulties of the person in front of them, as many older people do not reveal their feelings of distress and concentrate instead on reporting physical symptoms. Consequently, fewer than half of older people presenting to their general practitioners or primary care setting with significant mood disorders are actually diagnosed and fewer still receive treatment for their mental health difficulties (Conwell & Thompson, 2008). Ageist social attitudes which pervade contemporary Western society need to be challenged, so that suicide and suicidal behaviour in the older person can be adequately recognised and treated. Depression is not a normal feature of old age. Consequently, it is important that older people are aware of this and are encouraged to seek help when feeling distressed.

CASE SCENARIO 4.1

John is 79 years old. His wife of 52 years died recently after a long illness, which John helped nurse her through. He has three grown-up children, two of whom live abroad. His remaining son lives a two-hour car journey away and visits about once a month. John lives approximately three miles from his local village; however, his eyesight has deteriorated significantly over the past few months and as a result his GP was unable to declare him medically fit for a driving licence. As a result, John can no longer go to the village regularly. A nearby neighbour helps with shopping and brings him for medical appointments; however, apart from fairly regular but brief visits from this neighbour, John sees relatively few people from day-to-day. When his wife was ill, he had more frequent visits from his son in addition to regular calls from the community nurse providing support. On John's last visit to his GP for a review of his medication, he reports that he is staying in bed for most of the day and complained of feeling generally unwell. Although he did not disclose this to the GP, he has been thinking of ending his own life for a number of weeks and has made plans to do so through hoarding his prescribed cardiac medication.

- What factors do you think may have contributed to John feeling suicidal?
- What should the GP be aware of when assessing John?
- What help and supports may be offered to John?

Conclusion

Although there are many common risk factors that predispose to self-harm and suicidal behaviour amongst all age groups, it is clear from this chapter that each life stage has age-specific factors that may exert a particular influence on suicidal and self-harm behaviour. Many of these factors are stressful life events that may act as trigger factors, particularly in those already predisposed to mental health problems such as depression. Understanding the factors that make people vulnerable to self-harm and suicidal behaviour at different times in their lives provides the opportunity for additional suicide and self-harm prevention initiatives to be tailored to specific age groups.

REFLECTIVE QUESTIONS

1. What are the main risk factors associated with self-harm and suicidal behaviour in each of the four life stages?
2. How might knowledge of age-specific risk factors be useful in your work, give examples?
3. Think back to someone you worked with who experienced self-harm or suicidal behaviour. Can you identify if age-specific risk factors were evident in retrospect?
4. What age-specific risk factors would you like to learn more about and for what reasons?

REFERENCES

Australian Institute for Suicide Research and Prevention. (2003) *International Suicide Rates – Recent Trends and Implications for Australia.* Canberra: Australian Government Department of Health and Ageing.

Butterworth, P., Gill, S.C., Rodgers, B., Anstey, K.J., Villamil, E. and Melzer, D. (2006) Retirement and mental health: Analysis of the Australian survey of mental health and well-being. *Social Science & Medicine,* 62(5): 1179–1191.

Chen, H., Cohen, P., Kasen, S., Johnson, J.G., Bereson, K. and Gordon, K. (2006) Impact of adolescent mental disorders and physical illness on quality of life 17 years later. *Archives of Pediatrics and Adolescent Medicine,* 160: 93–99.

Cleas, L., Houben, A., Vandereycken, W., Bijttebier, P. and Muehlenkamp, J. (2010) Brief report: The association between non-suicidal self-injury, self-concept and acquaintance with self-injurious peers in a sample of adolescents. *Journal of Adoelscence,* 33: 775–778.

Conwell, Y. and Duberstein, P. (2005) Suicide in older adults: determinants of risk and opportunities for prevention. In Hawton, K. (ed.) *Prevention and Treatment of Suicidal Behaviour: From Science to Practice.* Oxford: Oxford University Press.

Conwell, Y. and Thompson, C. (2008) Suicidal behavior in elders. *Psychiatric Clinics of North America,* 31(2): 333–356.

De Leo, D. and Arnautovska, U. (2011) Prevention and treatment of suicidality in old age. In O'Connor. R.C., Platt, S. and Gordon, J. (eds.) *International Handbook of Suicide Prevention. Research, Policy and Practice.* West Sussex: Wiley-Blackwell.

Erlangsen, A., Nordentoft, M., Conwell, Y., Waern, M., De Leo, D., Lindner, R., Oyama, H., Sakashita, T., Andersen-Ranberg, K., Quinnett, P., Draper, B., Lapierre, S. (2011) Key considerations for preventing suicide in older adults. *Crisis,* 32(2): 106–109.

Flouri, E. and Buchanan, A. (2002) The protective role of parental involvement in adolescent suicide. *Crisis,* 23(1): 17–22.

Freake, H., Barley, V. and Kent, G. (2007) Adoelscents' views of helping professionals: A review of the literature. *Journal of Adolescence,* 30: 639–653.

Freuchen, A., Kjelsberg, E. and Grobolt, B. (2012) Suicide or accident? A Psychological autopsy study of suicide in youths under the age of 16 compared to deaths labelled as accidents. *Child & Adolescent Psychiatry & Mental Health,* 6: 30. http://www.capmh.com/content/6/1/30.

Hawton, K., O'Grady, J., Osborn, M. and Cole D. (1982) Adolescents who take overdoses: Their characteristics, problems and contacts with helping agencies. *British Journal of Psychiatry,* 140: 124–131.

Hawton, K., Fagg, J., Simkin, S., Bale, B. and Bond, A. (2000) Deliberate self-harm in adolescents in Oxford, 1985–1995. *Journal of Adolescence,* 23: 47–55.

Hawton, K., Rodham, K., Evans, E. and Weatherall, W. (2002) Deliberate self harm in adolescents: self report survey in schools in England. *British Medical Journal,* 325(7374): 1207–1211.

Hawton, K. and James, A. (2005) Suicide and deliberate self harm in young people. *British Medical Journal,* 330: 891–894.

Hawton, K., Rodham, K. and Evans, E. (2006) *By Their Own Young Hand. Deliberate Self-Harm and Suicidal Ideas in Adolescents.* London: Jessica Kingsley Publishers.

Hawton, K. and Harris, L. (2006) Deliberate self-harm in people aged 60 and over: Characteristics and outcome of a 20-year cohort. *International Journal of Geriatric Psychiatry,* 21(6): 572–581.

Hawton, K. and Harris, L. (2008) The changing gender ratio in occurrence of deliberate self-harm across the lifecycle. *Crisis,* 29(1): 4–10.

Hawton, K., Saunders, K.E.A. and O'Connor, R.C. (2012) Self-harm and suicide in adolescents. *Lancet,* 379: 2373–2382.

Hepp, U., Stulz, N., Unger-Koppel, J. & Ajdacic-Gross, V. (2012) Methods of suicide used by children and adolescents. *European Child and Adolescent Psychiatry,* 21(2): 67–73.

Hilt, L.M., Nock, M.K., Lloyd-Richardson, E.E. and Prinstein, M.J. (2008) Longitudinal study of nonsuicidal self-injury among young adolescents. *Journal of Early Adolescence,* 28(3): 455–469.

Joiner, T.E. (2003) Contagion of suicidal symptoms as a function of assortative relating and shared relationship stress in college roommates. *Journal of Adolescence,* 26: 495–504.

Kjaer, T.K., Jensen, A., Dalton, S. Johansen, C., Schmiedel, S. and Kjaer, S. (2011) Suicide in Danish women evaluated for fertility problems. *Human Reproduction,* 26(9): 2401–2407.

Klonsky, E.D. and Olino, T.M. (2008) Identifying clinically distinct subgroups of self-injurers among young adults: A latent class analysis. *Journal of Consulting and Clinical Psychology,* 76(1): 22–27.

Mayock, P., Bryan, A., Carr, N. and Kitching, K. (2008) *Supporting LGBT Lives: A Study of Mental Health and Well-Being.* Dublin: GLEN and BeLong To.

Macnab, A.J., Deevska, M., Gagnon, F., Cannon, W.G. & Andrew, T. (2009) Asphyxial games or 'the choking game': a potentially fatal risk behaviour. *Injury Prevention,* 15: 45–49.

McMahon, E.M., Reulbach, U., Corcoran, P., Keeley, H.S., Perry, I.J. and Arensman, E. (2010) Factors associated with deliberate self-harm among Irish adolescents. *Psychological Medicine,* 40(11): 1811–1819.

Meland, E., Rydning, J.H., Lobben, S., Breidablik, H.J. and Ekeland, T.J. (2010) Emotional, self-conceptual, and relational characteristics of bullies and the bullied. *Scandinavian Journal of Public Health,* 38: 359–367.

Mishara, B. (1999) Conceptions of death and suicide in children ages 6–12 and their implications for suicide prevention. *Suicide and Life-threatening Behavior,* 29(2): 105–118.

Montano, C.B. (1999) Primary care issues related to the treatment of depression in elderly patients. *Journal of Clinical Psychiatry,* 60(Suppl 20): 45–51.

Moran, P., Coffey, C., Romaniuk, H., Olsson, C., Borschmand, R., Carlin, J.B. and Patton, G.C. (2012) The natural history of self-harm from adolescence to young adulthood: a population based cohort study. *Lancet,* 379: 236–243.

Griffin, E., Arensman, A., Corcoran, P., Wall, A., Williamson, E. & Perry, I. (2014) *National Registry of Deliberate Self Harm Ireland: Annual Report 20132.* Cork: National Suicide Research Foundation.

Ougrin, D. and Latif, S. (2011) Specific psychological treatment versus treatment as usual in adolescents with self-harm. *Crisis,* 32(2): 74–80.

Portzky, G. and van Heeringen, K. (2007) Deliberate self-harm in adolescents. *Current Opinion in Psychiatry,* 20: 337–342.

Portzky, G., De Wilde, E-J. and van Heeringen, K. (2008) Deliberate self-harm in young people: Differences in prevalence and risk factors between The Netherlands and Belgium. *European Journal of Child and Adolescent Psychiatry,* 17: 179–186.

Scoliers, G., Portzky, G., Madge, N., Hewitt, A., Hawton, K., Jan de Wilde, E., Ystgaard, M., Arensman, E., De Leo, D., Fekete, S. and van Heeringen, K. (2009). Reasons for adolescent deliberate self-harm: A cry of pain and/or a cry for help? *Social Psychiatry and Psychiatric Epidemiology,* 44: 601–607.

Smyth, C., MacLachlan, M. and Clare, A. (2003) *Cultivating Suicide? Destruction of Self in a Changing Ireland.* Liffey Press: Dublin.

Stillion, J.M. and McDowell, E.E. (1996) *Suicide Across the Life Span.* 2nd ed. Washington DC: Taylor & Francis.

Tishler, C.L., StaatS Reiss, N. and Rhodes, A.R. (2007) Suicidal behavior in children younger than twelve: A diagnostic challenge for emergency department personnel. *Academic Emergency Medicine,* 14: 810–818.

Tobias, M., Kokaura, J., Gerritsen, S. and Templeton, R. (2010) The health of children in sole-parent families in New Zealand: Results of a population-based cross-sectional survey. *Australian and New Zealand Journal of Public Health,* 34(3): 274–280.

Usall, J., Pinto-Meza, A., Fernandez, A., de Graaf, R., Demyttenaere, K., Alonso, J., de Girolamo, G., Lepine, JP., Kovess, V. and Horo, J.M. (2009) Suicide ideation across reproductive life cycle. Results from a European epidemiology study. *Journal of Affective Disorders,* 116(1): 144–147.

CHAPTER 5

Understanding and Responding to Self-Harm

Jean Morrissey

Introduction

Self-harm has received increasing awareness and attention among profession-als, workers and lay persons, yet at the same time, little information or training is available, which enables people to understand and respond more skilfully and effectively to people who self-harm. This chapter examines the nature of self-harm and addresses some of the issues involved from the perspective of those who are harming themselves, as well as the workers and helpers working in a variety of voluntary, health and community settings. Some guidance for addressing some of these issues will also be offered.

LEARNING OUTCOMES

By the end of this chapter, you should be better able to:

1. describe what is meant by self-harm;
2. identify your beliefs and attitudes towards people who self-harm;
3. outline some of the issues and challenges for the worker when responding to people who self-harm;
4. demonstrate an understanding of how different communication skills can be used to enhance the helping relationship and respond more effectively to people who self-harm.

The language of self-harm

Understanding self-harm is a complex endeavour for all concerned and is fur-ther compounded by the ongoing debate concerning the language used both in the literature and in the work setting. Over the last 50 years or so, both clinicians and researchers in this field have struggled to gain consensus about satisfactory terminology that will provide the most clarity and sensitivity to suicide-related and non-suicide-related thoughts and behaviours (Jacobson & Mould, 2007). Throughout the literature various terms are used, which are often used interchangeably to describe the same behaviour (Fairbairn, 1995; O'Connor et al., 2011). Terms commonly used include self-harm, self-injurious behaviour, deliberate self-harm (DSH), attempted suicide, suicidal behaviour and non-suicidal self-injury. Many of these terms are used interchangeably; it is therefore important for those who work with people who self-harm to have a good understanding about how the following behaviours are defined, and more importantly how they might be understood in the work setting. Each of these terms will be briefly explained.

Self-harm

'Self-harm' is the term most widely used, largely due to the fact that it is the term used in the National Institute for Health and Clinical Excellence (NICE) (2004) guidelines, and encompasses both self-poisoning and self-injury. Defining self-harm is not an easy task; from a broad perspective self-harm can be used as an umbrella term to include a wide variety of self-injurious or health-impairing behaviours that may be incorporated into the lifestyle of many people, for example, smoking or binge drinking. Alternatively self-harm can be by omission, for example not wearing a seat belt or having unprotected sex (Pembroke, 1996; Turp, 1999, 2003). As such, self-harming behaviours can be viewed along a continuum ranging from self-care and at the other end of the spectrum suicide, which can be viewed as an act of self-harm (Babiker & Arnold, 1997; Turp, 2003). Notwithstanding the above, the more recent NICE (2011) guidelines on longer-term management of self-harm provide the following definition: 'any act of self-poisoning or self-injury carried out by an individual irrespective of motivation. This commonly involves self-poisoning with medication or self-injury with self-cutting' (NICE, 2011: 4).

Self-harming behaviours can include the following:

- scalding;
- burning;
- hitting;
- scratching;
- hair pulling;
- swallowing poisonous substances or objects.

Self-harm: Self-injury

Self-harm and self-injury are often used interchangeably. Self-injury can be described as 'an intentional self-inflicted attack(s) on the body, without suicidal intent, and for purposes not socially or culturally sanctioned' (Klonsky & Muehlenkamp, 2007: 1045). As with self-harm, self-injury is a complex and personal experience and may present in various ways; the most common forms include self-cutting or self-burning, usually of the arms and hands, sometimes the legs and less commonly the face. People may also injure themselves by scratching, biting, picking and occasionally inserting sharp objects under the skin. Less common methods include tying ligatures, pulling out one's hair and scrubbing oneself so hard (sometimes using cleansers such as bleach) as to cause abrasion (Duffy, 2009). Although different meanings underlie the terms 'self-injury' and 'self-harm', each refers to some degree of harmfulness to the body. According to Babiker and Arnold (1997: 2), 'self-injury is one part of a large repertoire of behaviours that involve the body in the expression of distress within the individual'. For a more expansive discussion on the range of behaviours involving harm to the body, see Babiker and Arnold (1997: 1–17).

Deliberate self-harm

Historically, the term 'deliberate self-harm' (DSH) was commonly used; however, more recently the prefix 'deliberate' has been dropped largely due to criticism by some writers in the field for its pejorative, accusatory overtones and therefore considered to be insensitive and inappropriate. In addition, the NICE (2004) guidelines on the short-term management of self-harm acknowledged that for some people they feel as if they have no choice or no other option than to self-harm, and for others the self-harm occurs in a dissociative state. This view is strongly supported by service users and experts by experience (Pembroke, 1996; Shaw & Shaw, 2007). Other terms used to describe a person's self-harm and often laden with value judgements may include descriptions such as 'superficial', 'not serious', 'non-life threatening', which can alienate the person who is self-harming. Furthermore, such terms offer no meaning or value and are often unhelpful for all concerned. It is for such reasons that Silverman (2006) argues that the term 'deliberate self-harm' should be removed from this lexicon.

Non-suicidal self-injury (NSSI)

In the United States, the term 'non-suicidal self-injury' (NSSI) as opposed to self-harm is commonly used to describe behaviours that include direct, deliberate self-inflicted destruction of one's own body tissue in the absence of suicidal intent and the exclusion of practices accepted as cultural norms (Favazza, 1987, 2012).

Self-harm: Suicide overlap?

The term 'self-harm' is now preferred over 'attempted suicide' in that not all individuals who self-harm tend to complete suicide. In the literature, there is a general consensus that self-harm and suicidal behaviour differ; the key difference being that in attempted suicide the person intends to kill himself/herself, but in self-harm the person does not (Tantam & Whitaker, 1992). As Babiker and Arnold (1997: 2) succinctly differentiate, 'self-injury [*self-harm*, my italics] continues the discourse of a person's life, whereas a suicide attempt separates the person from the discourse, removing the individual from their awareness or from being'. However, the significant differences between act(s) of self-harm and behaviour(s) that are suicidal in nature are not only differences in the outcome (Turp, 2003). Other factors grounded in empirical research inform the differentiation debate between self-harm and suicidal behaviour. These include methods, cognitions, aftermath, demographics and prevalence (Hawton, 2000), which will be addressed later in the chapter. Notwithstanding the above differences, suicide is often conflated with self-harm both in the literature and in clinical practice, wherein self-harm is viewed as an 'unsuccessful' or 'failed suicide attempt' and that it will lead on to a 'successful suicide' (Shaw, 2002). This understanding of self-harm contributes to high levels of anxiety and contempt towards people who self-harm, and who are often viewed as 'not genuinely' depressed or suicidal.

Some writers are critical of those who place 'these two distinct phenomena as one and the same, merely at different points of a continuum of lethality' (Cutcliffe & Stevenson, 2008: 154; Inckle, 2010; Turp, 2003). However, they also acknowledge that the line between suicidal and non-suicidal behaviour is often blurred and difficult to differentiate in individual cases. Furthermore, sadly there is evidence that some people who self-harm do go on to take their own lives. For the worker, knowing the presence or absence of intent to die is essential to distinguish a suicide attempt from self-harm (Ploderl et al., 2011); however, differentiating between forms of self-harm and suicidal behaviour is not always clear cut. Rosenberg et al. (1988) cautions that with respect to intent, 'absence of evidence is not evidence of absence' (1446). In addition, during times of distress the person may have 'complex, ambivalent and/or confused views of their exact intent' and as a result, the person who frequently self-harms may also at other times harm themselves with suicidal intent and often by using different means (Babiker & Arnold, 1997: 6). Therefore, workers, clinicians and others involved in helping the person need to be aware of the danger of considering self-harm as somehow less serious than suicide attempts, and more importantly, not responding to the profound despair and distress that it embodies for the person at that moment in time.

REFLECTIVE EXERCISE

1. What terms have you heard used in your area of work to describe self-harm?
2. What term do you use to describe self-harm?
3. How do you differentiate self-harm from suicidal behaviour?
4. In what way might different terminology be helpful or unhelpful to the person who self-harms?

Self-harm: Epidemiology

As stated in Chapter 1, self-harm is a major public health concern both in the United Kingdom and internationally; in the United Kingdom, much of the data collected on the prevalence of self-harm has been based on annual hospital attendance rates for intentional self-poisoning or self-injury, with a reported 200,000 episodes per year (Department of Health (DH), 2013). The United Kingdom has one of the highest rates of adult self-harm in Europe, at approximately 400 in every 100,000 population (Horrocks, 2002); the number of adults and adolescents who access emergency services in England following self-harm increased by 11% between 2007 and 2010 (Fernandes, 2011). However, self-harm is usually a secretive behaviour and many people who self-harm manage their wounds in private and do not seek professional/medical help, therefore figures on reported incidents do not accurately reveal prevalence estimates (Duffy, 2009).

Although international variation exists, self-harm is especially prevalent in young people, a group in whom rates of self-harm continue to increase (Mental Health Foundation, 2006). While there is an increased prevalence of suicide among males, in contrast women engage in self-harming more frequently than men in many Western countries and higher rates are generally found among young adults. As discussed in Chapter 4, although less common, self-harming behaviours are not limited to young people and is an indicator of very serious risk in older adults. See Murphy et al.'s (2012) study of 1177 older adults who attended three hospitals in the England with self-harm and found that 1.5% had died by suicide within a year of their presentation.

Similar to suicide, self-harm is not in itself a mental illness, but usually results from mental distress. People with current mental health problems are 20 times more likely to report having harmed themselves in the past (Mental Health Foundation, 2006). Self-harm is strongly associated with completed suicide; a history of self-harm has been identified as a significant risk factor for suicide with repeated episodes more likely to result in suicide than single episodes (Zahl & Hawton, 2004). Individuals who have self-harmed have a 30- to 200-fold increased risk of suicide in the year following an episode compared with individuals who have not self-harmed (Cooper et al., 2005). Research has shown that self-harm is not a singular occurrence; it often reoccurs and within a short period of time. Numerous factors are associated with repetition of self-harm including demographics, for example female and younger age. Methods of self-harm are heterogeneous, including acts described above; cutting is the most common followed by overdosing; however, since these methods are the hardest to hide they may not be the most common.

Functions of self-harm

'Self-harm is an expression of personal distress, not an illness, and there are many varied reasons to harm him or herself' (NICE, 2004: 7). The act of self-harming may hold many different meanings for each person who enacts the behaviour (Inkle, 2010; Turp, 2003). People who hurt themselves 'intentionally' do so because they feel that they need to, and that by carrying out the act itself it makes them feel better albeit temporary, and more able to cope. People who self-harm also report overwhelming feelings of emotional pain, distress, and hopelessness; as well as feelings of distress and a sense of feeling numb or lacking in emotional responses. This leads to the person finding an apparent solution, that is inflicting pain on his/her body (Gardner, 2002). For the person, inflicting pain may be considered to be the best or only solution and choice that he/she can make at that particular time. Indeed, Turp (2003) argues that the label 'self-harm' does a disservice when in fact the act of self-harm for some people is a strategy or coping mechanism to preserve rather than to destroy life. Self-harm can therefore be a means of helping the person to survive and keep alive.

For the person, self-harming behaviour is personal, meaningful and purposeful and it may serve many different functions. As well as helping with the regulation of emotions, self-harm can also help to regulate unpleasant self-states and help the person to:

- dumb-down feelings when feeling overwhelmed by anxiety, anger or guilt;
- feel something, for example pain during times of feeling disconnected from reality or depersonalisation (feeling unreal or in some extreme cases as if you are dead);
- manage unbearable feelings;
- gain a sense of control;
- cleanse self of self-hatred;
- provide self-comfort;
- communicate distress;
- punish self or others;
- provide a means of escapism;
- re-connect with self/ body;
- self-distract from difficult thoughts/memories;
- highlight an issue;
- influence outcomes;
- attention seeking – attention needing;
- provide a safety valve;
- cry for help.

The following fictitious cases illustrate different functions of self-harm at different times over the course of the lifespan.

CASE SCENARIO 5.1

Andrew, a 25-year-old mechanic, finds it difficult to talk about his self-harming behaviour. As a child he experienced being teased and called names for being overweight. Throughout his adolescence, he started to hit himself as a means of coping with his feelings. Now as an adult, Andrew sometimes returns to hitting himself at times of distress, particularly when he is anxious or fears that he might be criticised. He has recently started a relationship with Lily whom he likes a lot; however, he worries that he will 'mess it up', believing that he is 'not good enough for Lily'. Over time as the relationship develops, his anxiety increases and he struggles to cope with his fear of Lily ending the relationship. One evening prior to meeting Lily's family, he hit himself at work with a heavy tool and sustained a broken arm. He told Lily that he slipped and fell at work.

CASE SCENARIO 5.2

Zoe remembered her parents constantly fighting throughout her school years as if she wasn't present. She recalls always feeling anxious about never knowing when an argument might start; she recalls emotionally disengaging and cutting herself as a means of coping with her feelings and parents constant arguing. Now an adult and living away from home, she sometimes feels emotionally disconnected from people and at times of distress she returns to cutting wherein feeling pain and seeing herself bleed helps her to 'feel alive and present'.

CASE SCENARIO 5.3

Claire began to self-harm during her first year at university. Now in her forties, she has not self-harmed for many years, yet she keeps her 'self-harm kit' hidden in her bedroom. Knowing that she can access it if needed helps her to feel safe, particularly when she experiences suicidal thoughts.

REFLECTIVE QUESTIONS

Think of a person that you worked with or helped who self-harms and answer the following questions; illustrate your answer with examples.

1. How similar or different was the person's experience of self-harming behaviour to those in the above cases?
2. What function did the self-harming behaviour serve for the person in your area of work?
3. How did you respond to the person and why?
4. What were your colleagues' response to the person and why?
5. How might having a greater understanding of the varied functions of self-harm help you to work more effectively with the person?

Responses to people who self-harm

Self-harm is very complex and its meaning and function is unique to each person, one approach does not fit all. With self-harm, the whole point is you hurt yourself and not others; however, when you tell friends, relatives and professionals the solution becomes the problem and you hurt them (Turp, 2003). Self-harm can be a problem for many people and for many reasons, see Box 5.1. As such, the term 'self-harm' can trigger certain responses, thoughts, feelings assumptions and preconceptions for families, friends, workers and society that can impact on how people relate to people who self-harm. For those who come into contact with self-harm in a helping capacity, such responses have the potential to hinder the development of a trusting working relationship. In addition, the worker may struggle to understand the reasons underpinning the person's self-harming behaviour and as a result may find it difficult to respond in a helpful, compassionate and creative way. Furthermore, previous efforts by the worker to help may be refused or thwarted which can be frustrating. Also, for some helpers witnessing the reoccurrence of self-harm and within a short period of time can be very difficult to understand, particularly if the worker has invested a lot of time with the person and hoped and believed that the self-harming behaviour would cease. As a result, the worker may feel disappointed and find it difficult not to react in a judgemental, critical or even punitive manner.

BOX 5.1 WHO IS SELF-HARM A PROBLEM FOR AND WHY?

Who?	Why?
Professionals/Workers/Helpers	Lack of knowledge/experience/blamed
Family	Helplessness/Fear
Community	Not In My Back Yard (NIMBY)
Society	Stigma
Teachers	Lack of Time/Resources
Friends	Fear /Anger/Helplessness
Emergency Department staff	'Self-inflicted'/ Unknown
Other cultures	Risk to them self
Females and Males	Shame/Frustration
People of All ages Blame/Guilt	Denial
	Conflict of interest
	Limits of confidentiality
	Mandatory reporting
	Hopelessness

Unfortunately, people who have experienced self-harm (also referred to as self-injury) often feel they get a mixed response from service providers with whom they come in contact with (Pembroke, 1996). There is much evidence on the negative stereotyped attitudes about people who experience self-harm, resulting in men and women often feeling criticised, blamed, rejected or having their self-harm (distress) minimised by the use of pejorative terms such as 'slashers', 'cutters', 'attention-seeking', 'manipulative' and/or being labelled 'PDs' (Personality Disorder) (Babiker & Arnold, 1997; Inkle, 2010). Such terms do not describe the distress behind the self-harm; instead they become a label and stereotype the person who engages in self-harm behaviour, which can have serious and long-term implications for their care. The National Institute Health and Clinical Effectiveness (NICE) (2004: 7) acknowledged that the level of care provided in emergency services following an episode of self-harm was 'often unacceptable'. In addition, concern has also been raised not only about poor standards of care and management but also about the negative attitudes and feelings of irritation and anger received from frontline staff directly involved in the care of people who self-harm (NICE, 2004).

Against this background of negative attitudes, it is not surprising that staff in these services may therefore struggle to work effectively and with hope when working with the complex needs of this client group. The attitudes held by clinical staff towards people who harm themselves, together with their knowledge, skill and sensitivity about self-harm, are likely to influence their working relationship and hence the experiences and outcomes of those who self-harm. Inadequate training or lack of understanding about people who engage in self-harming behaviour may result in workers feeling unskilled and unsupported in their work, and as a result they may be reluctant to engage with people who self-harm or when necessary keep their contact to a minimum. The issue of self-harm and stigma is discussed in more detail in Chapter 2.

REFLECTIVE EXERCISE

- What do you think of when you hear the term 'self-harm'?
- What feelings have you experienced when working with a person who self-harmed, and for what reasons?
- How did you manage your feelings?
- What responses have you observed by other colleagues that have been helpful and/or unhelpful towards people who self-harm? Illustrate your answer with examples.
- In your area of work, in what way and for whom, is self-harm a problem?
- How might identifying this help you, your colleagues and those being helped who self-harm?

Self-harm and recovery: Understanding and responding to the person

Each person's experience of self-harm and recovery is personal and unique and will reflect in any given moment their experience of themselves and their world (Reeves, 2013). Self-harm is not a one-off behaviour; people may self-harm at different times and for different reasons over the course of their lifespan. People who self-harm may come into contact with or seek help from a variety of different professionals/workers within the community, for example, GPs, social workers, teachers, probation officers, youth workers, volunteers, Emergency Department nurses, community mental health nurses and many others; self-harm should therefore be seen as a multi-professional issue (Turp, 1999). Communication difficulties together with the interplay of previously held beliefs can reinforce the stigma associated with self-harm. Such misunderstandings and/or a lack of knowledge concerning the reasons underlying self-harm behaviour can give rise to barriers between the worker and the person. In order to work effectively, it is therefore essential for the worker/helper to demonstrate compassion, respect and be constantly mindful of the following issues from the outset so that people who self-harm experience something different from what they are often used to receiving.

The following principles are aimed to help the worker/helper to develop effective therapeutic engaging skills when responding and working with the person who self-harms.

Therapeutic principles

Working creatively and effectively with the person who self-harms needs to be based on a model of respect and facilitation as opposed to asking a series of standardised, impersonal interventions often used in the format of a checklist. There is no recipe, formula or one approach that fits all people who self-harm. Each interaction is different and will vary according to the context of the inter-action and nature of the helping relationship. Furthermore, talking with the person about his/her self-harm does not encourage the person to self-harm. The following communication skills/interventions and principles are intended to help the reader enhance his/her ability to work more creatively and effec-tively and are by no means exhaustive or conclusive. In order to work creatively and effectively the helper needs to:

- work within his/her professional competencies and values;
- state limits of confidentiality at the outset – this may depend on your place of work and policy and procedures, for example, concerning children/ adolescents; it is essential to be clear about such issues from the outset;
- adopt a 'person centred', respectful and non-judgemental approach;
- view the person beyond his/her self-harming behaviour, for example the person is a son, daughter, friend, teacher, mechanic;
- remain aware of your own beliefs, assumptions, expectations and how they might impact on your connecting and engaging with the person who self-harms;
- if you feel upset by the person's injuries, it may be best to be honest about this; while at the same time, it is essential that you state that you can deal with your own feelings and don't blame the person for causing your distress (see Chapter 7 for further discussion concerning self-care and supportive strategies);
- reflect continuously on your work – identify strengths, areas to develop and learning.

Listening

The ability to listen is one of the most important and helpful interventions; yet it is often the most challenging skill to undertake (Morrissey & Callaghan, 2011). To listen effectively the helper needs to consider the following:

- Offer an environment that is safe and private – the person needs to feel physically and emotionally safe at the outset.
- Acknowledge the therapeutic potency of active listening; being listened to can have a powerful therapeutic impact for the person who talks about their self-harming behaviour.

- Allow time to listen – be fully present with the person.
- Avoid interruptions – allow for silence and space for the person to think about what they are saying.
- Listen with your mind and body; use whole body to be fully present; be aware of eye contact, sitting and giving attention, body language, nodding/acknowledging without colluding or agreeing with the person.
- Be genuine and real when connecting with the person.
- Be mindful that being heard is an important way of validating the person particularly given that the person who self-harms has experienced chronic judgemental listening.
- Use listening prompts such as 'Mmm...', 'Yes'.
- Be minding of jumping to conclusions or providing solutions too early.

Facilitating person to tell his/her story

Facilitating the person to tell his/her story about their self-harming behaviour can be therapeutic for the person and help the person's recovery. For the helper, listening and hearing the person's story can also facilitate the process of engaging and seeing the person beyond their self-harming behaviour. In addition, it assists the helper to acquire a greater understanding of the function of the person's self-harming behaviour, which is both personal and unique for each person. In order to facilitate the person to tell his/her story the helper needs to consider the following:

- Provide time for the person to tell his/her story – the person may be embarrassed or afraid to talk about their self-harming behaviour for fear of criticism and/or rejection.
- Help the person to tell his/her story concerning the past, present and future; for example, 'tell me about the first time you self-harmed?', 'What does your self-harming behaviour – cutting – mean for you?'
- Avoid excessive use of questioning – in particular closed and 'why' questions, the latter sets up a defensive response and inhibits the person.
- Use exploratory statements, for example, 'Can you tell me about...', 'I am wondering whether....', 'Does this make sense?', 'I hear that are you saying....', 'Can I just check that I understand what you are saying...?'
- Be interested about the person rather than being curious about their behaviour, for example, 'You are interested in art, who is your favourite artist?', 'What type of things do you like to do to relax?'
- Use 'I' statements, for example, 'I am sorry that your experience in the Emergency Department was so difficult; you must feel very angry towards health professionals...'

Facilitating recovery

- Pace the interventions respectfully and in collaboration with the person.
- Be clear about your intentions, that is, to work with the person at his/her own pace.

- Do not offer solutions – guide person to his/her own solution, for example, 'What have you found helpful in the past?', 'What do you think you could do to slow down your feelings of distress?', 'Who could you ask for help?', 'What do you not want to do?', 'What's the most helpful thing for you when you are very distressed?', 'What's the least helpful thing for you when you are very distressed?'
- Avoid seeing cessation of self-harm as the only or most important goal. A person may make great progress in many ways and still need self-harm as a coping method for some time.
- Avoid using emotionally coercive statements to get the person to stop their self-harming behaviour, for example, 'Your parents are so worried about you – could you stop cutting for them?', 'You have a very caring family and they worry about you so much; have you thought about how your cutting affects them?'
- Avoid the use of terms such as 'you should', 'you must'.
- Support the person in beginning to take steps to keep safe and to reduce his/her self-harm – if he/she wishes to. For example, 'if you are scared that you are going to hurt yourself self after . . . , could you avoid drinking . . . ?'
- Acknowledge (genuinely) the person's strengths for example, 'I know it is difficult for you to ask for help; yet you did it today'.

REFLECTIVE EXERCISE

Reflecting on the above therapeutic engagement skills answer the following questions:

1. Which of the above do you consider yourself to be the most skilled when responding/working with the person who self-harms. Give examples.
2. Which of the above do you consider the most challenging when responding to a client/ person who self-harms and for what reasons? Give examples.
3. Identify two therapeutic engaging skills/interventions that you would like to develop further to help you to be more effective when responding/working with the person who self-harms.

Self-harm support groups and resources

There are many groups and services for people who are struggling with self-harm and their underlying causes. The following includes information concerning self-help groups, information and resources about self-harm and recovery.

http://www.selfinjurysupport.org.uk/
http://www.nshn.co.uk – National Self Harm Network
http://www.recoveryourlife.com/

Conclusion

Understanding self-harm is a complex endeavour for all concerned and is further compounded by the ongoing debate concerning the language used in both the literature and work setting. In addition this confusion still remains about what exactly constitutes self-harming behaviour. The nature of self-harm and some of the issues involved, including the workers' beliefs and assumptions need to be given serious consideration so that they can adopt a more open, compassionate and non-judgemental approach towards those who self-harm.

REFLECTIVE QUESTIONS

1. What is your understanding of self-harm?
2. In your experience, in what ways and for whom is self-harm a problem? How might identifying this help you in your area of work?
3. Reflecting on your own work experience, have you ever experienced a situation whereby your own values or position on a client's self-harming behaviour challenged you in your work with this person? If so, what was the issue and how did you reconcile it?
4. In your area of work, identify three things that you could do to help someone who is experiencing thoughts of self-harm.

REFERENCES

Babiker, G. and Arnold, L. (1997) *The Language of Injury: Comprehending Self-Mutilation.* Leicester: BPS Books.

Cooper J., Kapur, N., Webb R., Lawlor M. Guthrie E., Mackway-Jones K. and Appleby, L. (2005) Suicide after deliberate self-harm: A 4-year cohort study. *American Journal of Psychiatry,* 162: 297–303.

Cutcliffe, J. and Stevenson, C. (2008) A critique of Anderson's and Jenkins' article: 'The national suicide prevention strategy for England: The reality of a national strategy for the nursing profession'. *Journal of Psychiatric and Mental Health Nursing,* 15: 154–160.

Department of Health. (2013) Multi-centre study of Self Harm in England. Web site accessed September 2013.

Duffy, D.F. (2009) Self-injury. *Psychiatry,* 5: 263–265.

Fairbairn, G.J. (1995) *Contemplating Suicide: The Language and Ethics of Self Harm.* London, Routledge.

Favazza, A.R. (1987) *Bodies Under Siege.* Baltimore, MD: John Hopkins University Press.

Favazza, A.R. (2012) Nonsuicidal self-injury: How categorization guides treatment. *Current Psychiatry,* 11: 21–26.

Fernandes, A. (2011) *Guidance for Commissioning Integrated Urgent and Emergency Care. A 'Whole System' Approach.* RCGP Centre for Commissioning.

Gardner, F. (2002) *Self-Harm a Psychotherapeutic Approach.* Hove, UK: Brunner Routledge.

Hawton, K. (2000) Deliberate self-harm. *Medicine,* 28(5): 83–86.

Horrocks, J. (2002) Self-poisoning and self-injury in adults. *Clinical Medicine,* 2(6): 509–512.

Inckle, K. (2010) *Flesh Wounds? New Ways of Understanding Self-Injury*, Ross-on-Wye: PCCS Books.

Jacobson, C.M. and Gould M. (2007) The epidemiology and phenomenology of non-suicidal self-injurious behavior among adolescents: A critical review of the literature. *Archives of Suicide Research*, 11: 129–147.

Klonsky, E.D. and Muehlenkamp, J.J. (2007) Self-injury: A research review for the practitioner. *Journal of Clinical Psychology*, 63: 1045–1056.

Mental Health Foundation. (2006) *Truth Hurt Report of the National Inquiry into Self-harm among Young People Fact or Fiction?* London: Mental Health Foundation.

Murphy, E., Kapur, N., Webb R., Purandare, N., Hawton, K. and Bergen, H. (2012) Risk factors for repetition and suicide following self-harm in older adults: Multicentre cohort study. *British Journal of Psychiatry*, 200: 399–404.

National Institute for Health and Clinical Excellence. (NICE) (2004) *Self-harm: The Short-Term Physical and Psychological Management and Secondary Prevention of Self-Harm in Primary and Secondary Care (NICE Clinical Guidance 16)*. London: National Institute for Health and Clinical Excellence.

National Institute for Health and Clinical Excellence. (NICE) (2011) *Self-harm: Longer–term Management (Clinical Guideline CG 133)*. Manchester: National Institute for Health and Clinical Excellence.

Morrissey, J. and Callaghan, P. (2011) *Communication Skills for Mental Health Nurses*. Berkshire: Open University Press.

O'Connor, R. Platt, S. and Gordon J. (2011) *International Handbook of Suicide Prevention Research, Policy and Practice*. Chichester, West Sussex: Wiley-Blackwell.

Pembroke, L. (1996) 'Introduction' and 'Louise Roxanne Pembroke'. In Pembroke, L. (ed.) *Self-Harm: Perspectives from Personal Experience*. London: Survivors Speak Out.

Ploderl, M., Kralovec, K., Yazdi, K. and Fartacek. (2011) A closer look at self-reported suicide attempts: False positives and false negatives. *Suicide and Life-Threatening Behavior*, 41(1): 1–5.

Reeves A. (2013) *Challenges in Counselling: Self-harm*. London: Hodder Education..

Rosenberg, M.L., Davidson, L.E., Smith, J.C., Berman, A.L., Buzbee, H., Gantner, G., Gay G.A., Moore-Lewis, B., Mills D.H., Murray, D., O'Carroll, & P.W. and Jobes, D. (1988) Operational criteria for the determination of suicide. *Journal of Forensics Sciences*, 32: 1445–1455.

Shaw, S.N. (2002) Shifting conversations on girl's and women's self-injury: An analysis of clinical literature in historical context. *Feminism and Psychology*, 12(2): 191–219

Shaw, C. and Shaw, T. (2007) a Dialogue of hope and survival. In Spandler, H. and Warner, S. (eds.) *Beyond Fear and Control: Working with Young People Who Self-Harm*. Ross-on-Wye: PCCS Books.

Silverman, M.M. (2006) The language of suicidology. *Suicide and Life-Threatening Behavior*, 36: 519–532.

Tantam, D. and Whitaker, J. (1992) Personality disorder and self-wounding. *British Journal of Psychiatry*, 161: 451–464.

Turp, M. (1999) Encountering self-harm in psychotheray and counselling practice. *British Journal of Psychotherapy*, 15(3): 165–177.

Turp, M. (2003) *Hidden Self–Harm: Narratives from Psychotherapy*. London: Jessica Kingsley.

Zahl, D.L. and Hawton, K. (2004) Repetition of deliberate self-harm and subsequent suicide risk: Long-term follow-up study of 11, 583 patients. *British Journal of Psychiatry*, 185: 70–75.

CHAPTER 6

Communicating with People Who Are Suicidal

Jean Morrissey

Introduction

Communication is essential for all therapeutic/helping relationships and in particular when engaging with people who are suicidal. The knowledge and interpersonal skills that the worker uses to communicate are essential aspects of helping to prevent the immediate risk of suicidal behaviour, while at the same time facilitating the development of a positive helping relationship. For the worker, this requires the use of a range of appropriate and effective communication as well as engagement skills. This chapter presents some of the interpersonal skills and interventions that can be used to help prevent the immediate risk of suicidal behaviour. The chapter will provide examples to illustrate how the different skills can be used in practice.

LEARNING OUTCOMES

By the end of this chapter, you should be better able to:

1. describe how your beliefs and attitudes about suicide might impact on your interventions with the suicidal person;
2. identify the characteristics necessary to facilitate the development of a positive helping relationship;
3. demonstrate an understanding of how communication skills/interventions can be used to help assess and prevent the immediate risk of suicidal behaviour;
4. apply interpersonal skills and interventions to help the person who is suicidal in the work setting.

Connecting with the suicidal person

As stated at the outset of the book, the extent of suicide has become a serious public health issue and a major global cause for concern (Fleischmann & Shekhar, 2013). Suicide and suicidal behaviour affect many people directly, in both a personal and professional capacity. For those working in mental health and other helping services, suicide prevention is obviously a priority. Being able to connect, engage and communicate with people who are expressing suicidal thoughts or behaviours is critical to maintain and promote the person's safety and well-being. However, before being able to engage and communicate therapeutically with the person, it is important that the worker is aware of his/her beliefs and opinions about suicide and how they might influence their reactions.

Beliefs and attitudes about suicide

Over the years, societal beliefs and attitudes about suicide have varied tremendously; in many countries, suicide is no longer considered either a crime or a sin (O'Connor et al., 2011). Notwithstanding such significant changes, suicide remains a complex, emotive and difficult topic that produces a wide range of attitudes and responses from people, some of which may be pejorative and value-laden. In addition, the stigma associated with suicide, as discussed in Chapter 2, can influence people's beliefs and opinions about suicide, which can differ between and within helpers, institutions, societies and persons at risk of suicide. Such diverse views may influence not only how workers respond to the suicidal person but also whether people at risk of suicide ask for help or tell people how they are feeling. Negative reactions by helpers can cause a person to feel that the worker is unsympathetic, unconcerned and uncaring, which is likely to have a detrimental impact on the person's mental state (Hawton & van Heeringen, 2009). This in turn can put the therapeutic/helping relationship at risk and at the same time be detrimental to the person's immediate safety and long-term recovery (Royal College of Psychiatrists, 2010).

As a subject, suicide rarely leaves people in a neutral position (Reeves, 2012: 541); it is therefore likely that workers' views about suicide will be present in their therapeutic/helping interactions. Different beliefs about suicide can influence how a worker will respond to the disclosure of the possibility of suicide (Reeves, 2012). Being aware of one's opinions and feelings about suicide is essential in order to be able to listen to the beliefs and views of the person who is suicidal. Furthermore, having an awareness of such views can also help the worker to identify and manage his/her beliefs and feelings that might hinder their willingness and ability to engage and provide first-aid help to the person at risk.

Misconceptions and myths about suicide

In the context of helping, workers may be exposed to many different beliefs or misconceptions about suicide. Such beliefs or ideas about suicide are often a reflection of a much wider societal view and can become so embedded with little evidence or logic to support them that they become common misconceptions or 'myths'. The Irish Association of Suicidology (IAS) (2013) identified the following common 'myths' about suicide:

1. Most suicides occur with little or no warning.
2. Most suicides are caused by one single traumatic event.

3. Those who talk about suicide are the least likely to attempt it.
4. Talking about suicide encourages it.
5. If someone is going to complete suicide there is nothing you can do about it.
6. Suicidal people are fully intent on dying. They will do it eventually.
7. Suicide attempts are just cries for help – it's a form of attention seeking.
8. Only mentally ill/clinically depressed people make serious attempts at suicide.
9. Once a person is suicidal, they are forever suicidal.
10. Suicide can be relief not just for the individual but also for those that surround the person.

Some of the above myths will be discussed further in relation to their impact on conducting a suicide risk assessment. For the interested reader, coverage of the facts concerning such misconceptions about suicide is available at www .ias.ie.

Helpers' responses to suicide

Working with the suicidal person evokes a wide range of feelings, often occurring at the same time. For many workers, the presence of a discussion about suicide can be experienced as challenging and anxiety provoking. This can apply to both experienced and inexperienced workers. Reeves and Mintz's (2001) small study found that counsellors and psychotherapists with varying post-qualifying experience found it difficult when working with clients who were potentially suicidal and as a result did not explore with the client the meaning of his/her suicidal thoughts or consider the degree of intent and the level of risk. The range of responses experienced by workers is often underpinned by certain beliefs as illustrated in Table 6.1.

Table 6.1   Responses and beliefs to the suicidal person

Responses	Beliefs
Panic	I don't know what to do to help, I'm just a support worker and I'm not trained to deal with this type of situation.
Fear	I am afraid, what if I try to help the person and then they harm or kill themselves.
Frustration	I am busy now; I don't have time now to talk to the person about this.
Anger	I don't know what else to do; I have done all I can to help.
Resentment	I feel I am being used; the person is just looking for attention – it's doesn't seem really serious to me.

REFLECTIVE EXERCISE

The following exercise is aimed at helping you to identify your own views/beliefs and feelings about suicide and suicidal behaviour; illustrate your answer with examples.

1. What are your beliefs about suicide?
2. What has influenced your beliefs about suicide?
3. Has your beliefs changed over time, if so, in what way?
4. In what way are your beliefs about suicide the same or different from your family, friends, work colleagues or society?
5. What feelings does suicide evoke in you as a helper?
6. Have you ever experienced feeling angry/frustrated/disappointed/anxious when working with a person who expressed suicidal thoughts, if so for what reasons?
7. How do you manage your feelings when working with a person who is expressing suicidal thoughts?
8. What *myths* or misconceptions about suicide have you heard in your area of work?
9. Which of the myths identified above have you heard among your family/friends/colleagues or society?
10. What responses have you observed by other colleagues that have been helpful or unhelpful towards a person who expressed suicidal intentions?

Establishing a helping relationship

Similar to any therapeutic/helping relationship, the relationship between the worker and the suicidal person is paramount (Briggs, 2008). One of the most important factors in preventing suicide is the presence of a supportive resource. The person at risk of suicide needs someone to connect with, particularly at the time when their feelings of hopelessness are strong (Reeves, 2012). In such instances, the person is likely to seek out and approach a worker whom they trust and feel able to connect with in some way. In fact in the context of helping, suicidal persons have a well-tuned radar, which can detect the extent of a helper's interest (Royal College of Psychiatrists, 2010). Having a positive attitude towards those who engage in suicidal behaviour is therefore crucial to achieving any meaningful engagement and interaction. Exploring with the client the meaning of their suicidal thoughts and behaviours requires the worker not only to be able to connect with the person but also to demonstrate a willingness and ability to develop and remain connected with the person at risk. However, establishing a helping relationship does not just happen or should be taken as a given; instead, it is built with care, compassion and underpinned with certain core values, which are essential, particularly if the worker wants to develop, maintain and sustain a positive, supportive and therapeutic/helpful relationship with the person (Morrissey & Callaghan, 2011). Notwithstanding this, each helping/therapeutic relationship is unique and may be influenced by many factors; for example, the context of the helping relationship, the length of time the worker and the person know each other and, as stated earlier, the worker's beliefs and responses towards the suicidal person.

In any context of helping, being faced with a situation whereby a person is expressing suicidal thoughts or behaviour can seem frightening and often lead the worker to consider a range of behaviours and actions that might fall beyond his/her capacity to work/help (Reeves, 2012). As stated earlier, such fears can apply to both experienced and inexperienced workers. One way to allay such fears is for workers to become familiar with their organisational policies, procedures and practices concerning issues of risk, in particular, those relating to persons at risk of suicide and self-harm. In most organisations, such policies are in place to guide the workers in their role and to ensure that those being helped are responded to appropriately (Reeves, 2013).

Principles and characteristics of a helping relationship

Every interaction with a suicidal person is an opportunity for the worker to intervene by engaging into a supporting relationship and offering help to reduce the person's distress and potentially to save a life at that time (Cole-King et al., 2013). A person-centred approach lies at the core of any helping relationship. Carl Rogers' (1961) person-centred approach believed that if helpers built relationships based on what he referred to as the three core conditions – genuineness, acceptance and empathy – then the people they were attempting to help would begin to understand aspects of themselves that were previously unknown to them. For example, the person who is in a potential suicide risk may begin to explore and understand his/her beliefs and reasons for wanting to harm themselves or die at that particular time. Although each core skill will be described separately, it is important to note that in practice all three core conditions are interrelated, for example, in the context of helping one cannot demonstrate empathy without being congruent and unconditional.

The core conditions are the following:

- Empathy
- Congruence
- Unconditional positive regard.

The skill of empathy

The skill of empathy is widely recognised as a key component for all therapeutic/helping relationships (Roth & Fonagy, 2005). Its use is advocated as a potent and powerful skill, which contributes to the achievement of effective outcomes for the person being helped. Larson and Yao (2005) argue that workers who are empathic and compassionate are more likely to encourage those being helped to disclose more about their concerns, symptoms and behaviour, which is ultimately more effective when helping the potentially suicidal person. At its simplest, empathy refers to 'the ability to perceive the world from another person's viewpoint and to take on that perspective while not losing one's own' (Stevenson, 2008: 112). According to Rogers (1961), this means that the empathetic helper will sense or pick up on the person's feelings but will not lose what he calls the 'as if' component, that is 'as if' you were the other person. When conveying empathy, the 'as if' factor helps to protect the worker from being overwhelmed by the emotions and distress of the person being helped. This then helps the worker to be able to 'step back' and be more objective when offering therapeutic help to the person in distress. Being empathic requires the worker not only to tune into what the person is saying and describing but also to be able to convey that understanding to the person.

In many everyday communications, a sympathetic response, that is an expression of concern, comfort or consolation, is conveyed by the worker with regard to the person's distress or situation. However, while empathy is not sympathy, expressing sympathy is a first-level empathetic response, which acknowledges and validates the person's situation and is therefore also recognised as important for connecting with the person and developing rapport and trust in all helping relationships (Freshwater, 2003). Examples of sympathetic responses are as follows:

I am really sorry to hear that you have had such a difficult time

I am sorry you feel so upset

I am sorry that things have been really hard for you recently

Conveying empathy

Conveying the skill of empathy and its various components can be a challenging task for the worker. Rogers (1990) admitted that he was not always able to achieve these qualities in the helping relationship. Therefore, similar to most acquired helping skills, learning how to use empathy effectively demands time, practice and the ability and willingness to reflect on one's application of the skill with different people in different contexts throughout one's working life. Since each person and helping relationship is unique, there are no universal or magical empathetic sentences that will meet the needs of all persons at risk of suicide; as with most therapeutic/helping skills, 'one size does not fit all' (Stevenson, 2008: 109).

REFLECTIVE EXERCISE

Think of a person that you worked with or helped who expressed suicidal thoughts or behaviour and answer the following questions; illustrate your answer with examples.

1. What challenges did you encounter listening to the person talk about suicidal intentions?
2. What feelings did it evoke for you at the time?
3. How did you respond to the person at the time?
4. On reflection, how might respond now – the same or differently and for what reasons?

Notwithstanding the challenges for workers, connecting with the person and conveying empathy is essential in order to help save lives and requires the worker to, or at best, make every effort to implement the following:

- Be fully present (physically and emotionally) with the person.
- Stay in the here-and-now with the person.
- Listen attentively, with interest and at the person's pace, to gain a deeper understanding of the person and his/her situation.
- Be mindful of the tone of your voice and your body language; for example, non-verbal behaviour, for example, facial expression, eye contact, posture should reflect what and how the message is being conveyed verbally.
- Acknowledge that you can never truly understand the person's experience, for example, 'I can only imagine how difficult it must feel for you at this moment, when you think everything is hopeless'.
- Be aware of your own thoughts (judgements) and feelings towards the person who is suicidal and how they might be hindering your ability to be fully present for the person.
- Stay with the person's frame of reference, that is his/her perspective and experience and not your thoughts, feelings and expectations.
- Check frequently with the person as to the accuracy of what you are sensing or picking up and be guided by the responses you receive; for example, Worker: 'so life has been so difficult for you of recent that you want to end it . . . because you think it will stop the emotional pain you are feeling, is that how it is for you?' Person: 'I don't want to die . . . . I just want the pain to go away; I am tired of feeling miserable'.
- Empathetic statements should be tentative and used sparingly; when overused they can sound very contrived, false and not real or genuine.

Examples of empathetic statements:

- 'You appear very distressed; I wonder if you are hurt by your father's response to your overdose?'
- 'I get the sense that things are really difficult for you and have been for a long time and that at this moment you cannot see any reason to live?'
- 'Listening to what you said, I get the sense that you have been hiding your fleeting thoughts about killing yourself for fear that your mum and dad would get very upset?'

Congruence

Another important core condition in the context of helping is congruence. Being congruent refers to the worker being genuine or real in their therapeutic/helping skills and relationships. This means that the worker relates to the person in a genuine manner and does not hide behind a uniform, medical jargon or the organisation. It means being as open and honest as possible with the other person about one's thoughts and feelings.

Unconditional positive regard

Unconditional Positive Regard (UPR) refers to accepting the person for who she/he is; no matter what his/her behaviour, feelings or condition is (Rogers, 1961). This means being non-judgemental and being able to demonstrate that acceptance to the person. This does not necessarily mean approving or accepting all behaviours; in fact, there may be some situations whereby the worker does not approve of the person's behaviour. In such situations, the worker strives towards separating the person from their behaviour and valuing them as an individual, which in practice can be challenging as illustrated in the following case.

CASE SCENARIO 6.1

Ruby is a senior counsellor working in a large school. Part of her role involves facilitating trainees from different helping professional backgrounds to get the most from their placement in an educational setting and maximise their professional learning. Ruby is particularly interested in helping trainees to develop their knowledge and practice especially concerning working with adolescents and young adults who are suicidal. On meeting Jade, a new trainee, Ruby asks her the following question. What issue(s) has been the most challenging for you to date and for what reason(s)? Jade stated, '...I am a mum of two teenage boys, yet I find it hard to empathise with some students particularly when they "threaten" suicide to manipulate their parents and cause them much distress. I think about how I would feel if it was one of my sons.' After some discussion, Jade acknowledged that she also found it hard to separate the behaviour from the person, for example, the taking of frequent overdoses. On reflection, she began to realise that she needed to 'tune in' more to what the person was saying and pay less attention to her own views and judgements about the person's behaviour.

Assessing the risk of suicide

As well as engaging into a compassionate, caring and trusting relationship, the worker also needs to undertake a comprehensive risk assessment with the potentially suicidal person. Suicide risk assessment and management are of major importance in reducing the risk of a completed suicide (Royal College of Psychiatrists, 2010). As described in Chapter 3, undertaking a suicide risk assessment requires the worker to be familiar with the evidence-based risk factors, warning signs and protective factors for suicide, all of which need to be taken seriously. Notwithstanding their importance, the worker also needs to be aware that just as each person has a different way of coping with stress, the person may also experience and behave differently when they are considering suicide. Therefore, appraising factors associated with a high risk of suicide also needs to be individually focussed as illustrated in the following case.

CASE SCENARIO 6.2

Rupert is a 54-year-old solicitor, married with two grown-up daughters, presented at the Emergency Department having taken a serious overdose. According to his daughter Libby, Robert is happily married, enjoys his job and has no financial difficulties. He has no history of mental illness and there is no known family history of depression or suicide. Libby is both shocked and distressed, and cannot understand why her dad might want to end his life.

CASE SCENARIO 6.3

Gertrude is an 84-year-old widow who lives alone in the country. Up until recently, she enjoyed a very active social life with various family members, friends and neighbours. Over the last six months, she has begun to notice that she tends to forget things. She fears that she might be getting Alzheimer's like her parents, whom she looked after for many years. She has begun to think about suicide before her health deteriorates further. She does not share her thoughts with her family or friends for fear that they might try to change her mind.

CASE SCENARIO 6.4

Krystal is a 20-year-old student who was recently discharged from hospital following a serious overdose. Krystal regrets her behaviour and feels embarrassed that she caused so much distress for her family. Krystal has a history of self-harming behaviour as a teenager but has not cut herself for the last year.

REFLECTIVE EXERCISE

Answer the following questions, illustrating your answer with examples.

1. What are the warning signs, risk factors and protective factors for suicide in each of the above cases?

When undertaking a suicide risk assessment, the person who is contemplating suicide or who has tried to take their life is likely to be feeling distressed at that time. Although it might seem frightening, the worker can help the distressed person by staying calm, acknowledging their current problem/distress and conveying acceptance, while at the same time provide the person privacy and offer a space to talk about their thoughts and feelings. The best caring response at that time is a non-judgemental approach and active listening (Cutcliffe & Stevenson, 2007). Listening actively is one of the most important helping interventions and means giving your full attention, physically, mentally and emotionally, to the person who is talking (Arnold & Underman Boggs, 2003). While listening to the person, the worker may be able to draw the person into a supportive relationship and away from self-destructive thoughts at that moment. This intervention can also provide a safe period of time until other forms of help can be obtained.

Suicide risk is determined by thoughts of death (suicidal intent), hope-lessness, the methods considered, development of a plan (the degree and seriousness of that intent), risk factors and specific warning signs (O'Connor et al., 2011). Although undertaking a suicide risk assessment can be poten-tially life-saving, the assessment is dependent on what the person chooses to disclose or not to the worker. For the worker, determining the level of suicide risk is reliant on the person's disclosure of their suicidal thoughts. Cole-King (2010) points out that such disclosure must not be underestimated, which in itself can act as a protective factor. However, while some people may talk openly about their suicidal thoughts, others may find it difficult and painful and will not talk about them or instead might refer to them through the use of metaphors or ambiguous statements. For example, the person might say:

'I just can't take it anymore ...'
'No one would miss me ..'
'I feel like I am stuck in a very black hole ...'
'I am causing my family so much worry'

It is important that the worker recognises and responds to such potential messages along with other things that he/she might observe and pick up, for example, the person's body language or change in behaviour, all of which might be invitations from the person to help prevent suicide. It is therefore important that the worker asks openly about suicide, for example:

- 'Have you ever thought about suicide?'
- 'Have you sometimes felt like harming yourself?'
- 'Have you thought about ending your life?'

Exploring the suicide question

For many workers, one of the biggest fears when working with the risk of suicide is that discussing suicidal thoughts may directly lead to an increased rate of suicide (Cole-King et al., 2013). As stated earlier, the belief that talking about suicide encourages it is a myth (IAS, 2013). If the person is experienc-ing suicidal thoughts, the worker needs to ask further questions to gain as much information as possible. Moreover, in order to undertake a comprehen-sive suicide risk assessment, it is essential that workers are not afraid of asking questions about suicidal thoughts and exploring the subject in depth. Given that many potentially suicidal people are reluctant to begin talking about sui-cide, workers must talk openly about it; in fact by doing so, it is more likely to reduce rather than increase the risk of suicide.

Asking suicide questions

When posing questions about suicide they should be clear, direct and unam-biguous. The most useful forms of questions are open-ended and begin with 'when?', 'what?', 'how?', 'who?' or 'where?' Asking an open-ended question invites a full descriptive response. The following questions are examples of how to gain as much information as possible about the person's suicidal thoughts and other relevant information when undertaking a comprehensive suicide risk. The questions are by no means intended to be exhaustive or prescriptive but instead aim to provide the general principles for the use of each skill presented. It is important to remember that when used in practice, they will be used together with the skills of listening actively and non-verbal communication (Table 6.2).

The following skills should at best be avoided:

- Closed questions: these limit the other person's options and often only allow a response of 'yes' or 'no', for example, 'Do you have suicidal thoughts?'
- Leading questions: these involve imposing your own perspective or being suggestive, for example, 'So you must have felt very upset after getting a diagnosis of depression?' rather than 'How did you feel after receiving a diagnosis of depression?'
- Why questions: these tends to invite an answer rather than a description or an exploration and the use of 'why' may appear interrogative and as a result may evoke a defensive response. For example, 'Why do want to end your life?' rather than 'What has happened that makes you want to end your life?'

For workers, the prediction of suicide evokes much anxiety and concern, yet it is fraught with difficulty and the level of accuracy (Briggs, 2008). Nevertheless, people communicating suicidal thoughts is often a cry for help; therefore any statement, a vague comment, a gesture, or a very small change in the person's typical behaviour must be taken seriously and met with compassion and a constructive response in order to engage positively with the person. If the worker can engage into a supportive helping relationship and help the person to talk about their thoughts and feelings, it can help them to look beyond their immediate situation and avail of potential short-term solutions and resources that are available and can be put into action.

REFLECTIVE EXERCISE

Reflecting on your suicide risk assessment skills, answer the following questions:

1. What do you consider the most challenging when communicating with a person who is expressing suicidal thoughts?
2. Identify two therapeutic engaging skills/interventions that you would like to develop further to help you to be more effective when undertaking a suicide risk assessment.

Table 6.2 Examples of suicide risk questions

Background and current problems	'What has happened recently [48 hours] that has led you to feel depressed ....? that has led you to take an overdose ....? that has led you to cut yourself ....?'
Suicidal thoughts: Nature of the suicidal thoughts, frequency, intensity, persistence.	'Have you ever thought about harming or killing yourself?' 'How long have you had these thoughts?' 'When did they start?' 'How often do you have these thoughts?' 'How do you feel when you have these thoughts?' 'What makes them worse?' 'Have you ever had these thoughts in the past?' 'Have you told anyone else about your suicidal thoughts?'
Degree of suicide intent – suicide plans	'If you were to take your own life, how would do it?' 'Have you made any plans about how you might kill yourself?' 'How would you get ... the tablets, rope?' 'Where would you do it?' 'Have you thought about a time?' 'What has stopped you from doing it ....?'
History of self-harm/suicide	'Have you ever tried to harm or kill yourself in the past?' 'What happened?' 'How did you feel after wards?' 'Did you think you needed help at that time, if so what help?' 'What help did you get at the time?' 'How useful was it?' 'How similar or different was that to how you are feeling currently?' 'Who knows that you tried to harm or kill yourself in the past?'
Perception of the future and any hopelessness	'How do see your future?' 'What would you like to happen in the future?' 'Using a scale of 1–10, with 1 being the best and 10 being the worst, how would you rate your feeling and thoughts about suicide at this moment?' 'What do you think could improve or help your rating?' 'What has given you hope in the past?' 'How has that changed?'
Ability to resist acting on their thoughts of suicide and self-harm	'What has helped you not to kill or harm yourself?' 'How could that help you now, if so, in what way?' 'If not, because ....?' 'How do you support yourself at difficult times?'
Reasons for living	'Who do you usually ask for help to get through a difficult time?' 'Are they available?'

Managing the risk of suicide

For many people, periods of feeling suicidal may be short-lived; while for others their suicidal thoughts might be always present, in fact knowing that they have the option to end their life may be enough to keep the person alive. Suicidal thoughts can and do also change over a very short period of time. Having undertaken a suicide risk assessment, the worker needs to appraise the person's responses and determine the extent of the person's suicide risk. Different actions will be taken by the worker depending on the seriousness of the person's suicidal thoughts and intent to die, together with their ability to delay a possible suicidal act and the presence of protective factors at that time. The worker may involve professional intervention with a possible admission to hospital or in some situations 'co-create' support to keep the patient safe in their home and community.

Developing a safety plan

Working collaboratively, the worker can help to develop a safety plan with the suicidal person, and in some situations with the person's permission engage his/her family/friends. A safety plan aims to keep the person safe during the immediate period and in the future by helping the person to connect with people close to them and in their community. Developing a safety plan requires time and the worker has to listen actively to the person, so that they can co-create a plan that is tailor-made to the individual's needs and resources at that time. The person should feel comfortable with their safety plan and agree to interventions outlined in it, particularly those concerning times when the person might feel the most vulnerable, for example at weekends or late at night. Table 6.3 identifies the specific issues that need to be identified when co-creating a safety plan along with examples of possible questions that can be asked by the worker.

Training

There are a range of training initiatives relating to suicide prevention and mental health promotion. The ASIST short training programme is designed to suit the needs for all kinds of caregivers/helpers including volunteers and is currently the most widely used and researched intervention training programme in the world. The following provides a brief outline of the programme; for further information, see www.livingworks.net/AS

ASIST: Applied Suicide Intervention Skills Training

ASIST is an internationally recognised skills awareness programme in suicide prevention. It was developed in the 1980s by a team of mental health professionals in the fields of psychiatry, psychology and social work, in collaboration with the state governments of Alberta and California. As a suicide prevention programme, it was developed in response to growing concern at the time about suicide in the region. Originally developed for the Canadian province of Alberta, Canada, since then the programme has been delivered through networks of registered trainers in Canada, the United States, Australia, Norway, Ireland and Scotland. The Canadian-based LivingWorks Education Inc is the central organisational body for ASIST.

ASIST is designed for all front-line care givers from all disciplines and occupational groups including the general public. The aim of the ASIST

Table 6.3 Developing a safety plan

Areas to identify	Questions
Early warning signs: physical, behaviour, thoughts, emotions, for example,	What warning signs do you get when you are distressed?
'I lose my appetite'; 'I get irritable with everyone'; 'I start to think about the negative things in my life'.	How can use this information to help you to keep safe? What could you do that would help when you ......? Who could you contact at that point?
Potential triggers: for example, 'I feel worse when I drink', 'I am on my own and I can't sleep'.	What helps you to drink more safely? For example reduce amount, type of drink, drink in group; eat before drinking? Which of the above could you do to keep yourself safe if you are drinking? What helps you to sleep at night?
Network of support: family, friends, professionals, community, voluntary agencies	Who is your network of support? Where are they? When are they available? How can they be contacted? What if . . . is not available, who can you contact then? Have you informed the person that you might contact them late at night?
Reasons for living	What has kept you from not harming yourself to date? What are the reasons you have kept living until now?
Resources/coping skills	What length of time could you feel safe? What helped you before to keep safe? What did you do then? Who did you contact?

workshop is to help caregivers/helpers to be more prepared and able to provide practical suicide first aid to persons at risk of suicidal behaviour. ASIST is a two-day intensive, interactive and practice focussed workshop designed to help helpers to recognise risk and learn how to intervene to prevent suicide. As an interactive workshop, participants examine their attitudes to suicide, learn how to recognise and review the risk of suicide and develop their skills through simulations and role-playing in order to become more ready, willing and able to help people at risk of suicide.

Conclusion

This chapter has outlined the different interpersonal skills that are used when communicating to the potentially suicidal person to help the person stay safe.

Being able and willing to engage into a positive compassionate helping relationship is paramount when working with the suicidal person. This requires the worker to be aware of his/her beliefs and opinions about suicide and to give serious consideration to how they might influence their reactions in order that they can adopt a compassionate and non-judgemental approach when working with the suicidal person.

REFLECTIVE QUESTIONS

1. How would you respond to a colleague who stated, 'people who talk about suicide never actually carry it out'?
2. Reflecting on your own work experience, have you ever experienced a situation whereby your own values or position on a client's suicidal behaviour challenged you in your work with this person? If so, what was the issue and how did you reconcile it?
3. How might the person who is suicidal know that you are listening actively to him?
4. What open questions would you ask to help a person to talk about their suicidal thoughts and intentions? Illustrate your answer with examples.

REFERENCES

Arnold, E. and Underman Boggs, K. (2003) *Interpersonal Relationships Professional Communication Skills for Nurses*. 4th ed. London: WB Saunders.

Briggs, S. (2008) Postvention: The impact of suicide and suicidal behaviour on family members, professionals and organisations. In *Relating to Self-Harm and Suicide Psychoanalytic Perspectives on Practice, Theory and Prevention*. London: Routledge, pp 224–237.

Cole-King, A. (2010) Suicide mitigation: Time for a more realistic approach. *British Journal of General Practice*, 60: 3–4.

Cole-King, A., Green, G., Gask L., Hines K. and Platt S. (2013) Suicide mitigation: A compassionate approach to suicide prevention. *Advances in Psychiatric Treatment*, 19: 276–283.

Cutcliffe, J.R. and Stevenson, C. (2007) *Care of the Suicidal Person*. London: Churchill Livingstone Elsevier.

Fleischmann, A. and Shekhar, S. (2013) Suicide prevention in the WHO Mental Health Gap Action Programme (mhGAP). *Crisis*, 34(5): 295–296.

Freshwater, D. (2003) *Counselling Skills for Nurses, Midwives and Health Visitors*. Maidenhead: Open University Press.

Hawton, K. and van Heeringen, K. (2009) Suicide. *Lancet*, 373: 1372–1381.

Larson, E.B. and Yao, Y. (2005) Clinical empathy as emotional labour in the patient-physician relationship. *JAMA*, 293: 1100–1106.

Morrissey, J. and Callaghan, P. (2011) *Communication Skills for Mental Health Nurses*. Berkshire: McGraw Hill-Open University Press.

O'Connor, R. Platt, S. and Gordon J. (2011) *International Handbook of Suicide Prevention Research, Policy and Practice*. Chichester, West Sussex: Wiley-Blackwell.

Reeves, A. (2012) Working with suicide and self-harm in counselling and psychotherapy. In C. Feltham and Horton I. (eds.) *The Sage Handbook of Counselling and Psychotherapy*. London: Sage, pp 539–544.

Reeves, A. (2013) *Challenges in Counselling: Self-harm*. London: Hodder Education.

Reeves, A. and Mintz, R. (2001) Counsellors' experiences of working with suicidal clients: An exploratory study. *Counselling and Psychotherapy Research*, 1(3): 172–176.

Rogers, C. (1961) *On Becoming a Person*. London: Constable.

Rogers, C. (1990) *A Way of Being*. Boston: Houghton Mifflin.

Roth, A. and Fonagy, P. (2005) *What Works for Whom? A Critical Review of Psychotherapy Research*. 2nd ed. New York: Guildford Press.

Royal College of Psychiatrists. (2010) *Self-Harm, Suicide and Risk: Helping People Who Self-Harm* (College Report CR1580). London: Royal College of Psychiatrists.

Stevenson, C. (2008) Therapeutic communication in mental health nursing. In Morrissey, J., Keogh, B. and Doyle, L. (eds.) *Psychiatric/Mental Health Nursing: An Irish Perspective*. Dublin: Gill & Macmillan.

The Irish Association of Suicidology (IAS). (2013) *Risk Factors & Myths about Suicide*. www.ias .ie Accessed 6 January 2013.

CHAPTER 7

Self-Care: Professional and Personal Considerations

Jean Morrissey

Indroduction

Working with people who are suicidal or self-harm means being exposed to intense and extreme emotions. In the context of helping, the need for workers to pay attention to their own well-being is paramount not only for the sake of themselves but also for their clients and work colleagues. This chapter will examine the role of self-care and its use in a therapeutic/helping setting. Examples of various strategies, which aim to help the worker identify his/her self-neglecting tendencies and to enhance their capacity to self-care, will also be outlined.

LEARNING OUTCOMES

By the end of this chapter, you should be better able to:

1. explain the concept of self-care;
2. identify factors that might precipitate periods of compromised self-care;
3. describe how self-care strategies can be implemented in different helping contexts;
4. demonstrate an understanding of how caring for self can be used to enhance effectiveness in the context of helping.

Understanding self-care: What is it?

Self-care is something that we regularly advocate and encourage, yet it is often overlooked or compromised when confronted with the daily demands of our professional/working and personal life (Reeves, 2010). The concept of self-care has received increasing attention and discussion in the literature, particularly in the psychotherapeutic literature and to a lesser degree in other helping disciplines, for example nursing (Smith, 1992). However, issues relating to self-care are complex. These issues are further compounded by the fact that the term 'self-care' is often used in different contexts as though there was a shared agreed meaning of the terminology used. It is therefore important to be explicit about what is understood by the term 'self-care' and more importantly how it is used in a work setting. In the field of helping, self-care for workers is a difficult concept to define; at its simplest, it refers to a form of thinking and behaving that involves achieving an optimal balance between self-care and other-care (Corey & Corey, 2011). It is essential for both the worker's ongoing professional and personal well-being and is an integral component for their work and professional identity.

Self-care is not a one-off event; it is an ongoing purposeful activity that is important throughout the person's working life and particularly during times of excessive stress when the workload is demanding in terms of either its volume and/or its emotional demands (Turp, 2003). While trainees or newly qualified workers might be more susceptible to emotional distress as a result of either their age, inexperience and/or the inherent demands of the work environment, it is incorrect to assume that experience alone precludes the need for self-care. Caring for oneself applies to all workers qualified and unqualified, senior and junior (Reeves, 2010). Furthermore, it is also important that self-care is not viewed as a luxury or as something 'extra' that only takes place if and when you have the time and resources (Barnett et al., 2006: 263). In fact, Norcross and Guy (2007) asserts that self-care is an 'ethical imperative' (14) for all workers in the field of helping and their helping relationships, so that those in the area of helping can maintain the provision and delivery of their work to the highest standard possible. When the practitioner or worker is not mindful of the ongoing need for self-care, other-care and relationships in the form of professional and at times personal may suffer (Barnett et al., 2006). The following case illustrates a worker's life-long commitment to self-care.

CASE SCENARIO 7.1

After the death by suicide of her younger sister over 20 years ago, Zadie decided to become a volunteer for a large charity, which provides 24-hour emotional support to anyone struggling to cope. Zadie works as a telephone counsellor two nights per week, and as an experienced volunteer, she also helps with the training of new volunteers. Reflecting on her own training as a volunteer, she recalls how her mentor Zack at that time stressed the importance of maintaining good self-care. Looking back, as a novice volunteer, she did not fully understand its significance and value at the time. Over the years however, she has learnt to appreciate the need to maintain good physical and emotional health in order to sustain her ability to work effectively. Zadie now echoes her former mentor's mantra to trainees about the importance of 'caring for self to care for others'.

REFLECTIVE QUESTIONS

1. What has this case highlighted to you about self-care?
2. When did you learn about the importance of self-care?
3. In what way do you demonstrate good self-care to your colleagues? Illustrate your answer with examples.

The workplace as a place of stress

Working with people who are suicidal and/or with self-harming behaviour may take place in various settings, for example an emergency department, remand centre, residential or community setting, and as such include workers from a range of voluntary and statutory agencies and/or disciplines. As many workers are employed in some kind of organisation, it is useful to reflect on the major sources of frustration and dissatisfaction that are likely to be part of the workplace and contribute to occupational stress. According to Corey and Corey (2011), sources of work-related stress fall into two categories: environmental and individual. In order to understand stress, it is therefore important to examine both the external realities that tend to produce stress and the ways in which the worker may contribute to the stress by their perceptions and responses. As the National Health Service (NHS) – one of the biggest employers of workers in the field of helping – moves towards outcome-focused practices and the increasing use of mechanisms such as 'payment by results' (PbR) (Department of Health [DH] Fund, 2010), workers are working in challenging and uncertain times, wherein they are required to face greater demands, higher expectations and accountability and, at times, a sense of isolation (DH, 2012). At the same time, as NHS Trusts, voluntary agencies and charities are required to make substantial savings; there are fewer workforce numbers, resources and support systems that are needed to provide adequate services. Against this background, workers may feel not valued by the organisation in which they are employed, yet they may still try to care for and work with individuals who present with complex, multi-layered and traumatic stories of distress (Corey & Corey, 2011). Working with people who are suicidal or self-harm requires time, patience and compassion. However, one major stress faced by many employees is the reality of having too much to do in too little time and, as a result, workers may try to make every effort to provide the level of care that is necessary in an unrealistically short time, often resulting in stress for both the helper and person being helped, as portrayed in the following example:

> ### CASE SCENARIO 7.2
>
> Ellie, an experienced nurse in a busy Emergency Department, often leaves work feeling dissatisfied, stressed and frustrated. Although she tries to spend as much time as possible listening to clients who present with self-harming behaviour talk about their thoughts, feelings and the issues that have contributed to their distress, she is aware that she often feels under pressure 'to hurry' when talking to them and/or their families, so that she can attend to other clients and the various tasks required before finishing her shift. She felt embarrassed when a client Claire recently said to her, '*I am sorry, I know you are very busy – I am sorry, I am taking so long – it's just . . . . it's so difficult for me to talk about my cutting*'.

REFLECTIVE QUESTION

1. In your area of helping, how might you feel under pressure when talking to clients who self-harm?

Other sources of stress that workers may encounter include aspects of the work environment itself, such as the lack of suitable and private rooms or spaces that are conducive to facilitating discussion between the worker and person in distress/or their families. In addition, while working with co-workers can be a source of support, this is often dependent on the quality of the working relationships with colleagues, for example some co-workers may be difficult to get along with because of their negative attitudes or behaviours, particularly towards persons who present with repeated self-harming behaviour as discussed in Chapter 5.

REFLECTIVE EXERCISE

The following exercise is designed to assist you with identifying and examining issues/incidents that you considered stressful in your area of work. Reflecting on your area of work, identify a particular issue/incident that you experienced as stressful in your area of work, and answer the following questions:

What was the issue?	*The issue was* ......
What were your thoughts and feelings about at the time?	*I thought that* .... *I felt* ......
How did you respond (or not)?	*I tried to* ......
What was useful about your response?	*It helped to reduce* ....
What was <u>not</u> useful about your response?	*I didn't ask* ....
What would you like to do differently in the future and why?	*I would first listen* .... *then do* ......
What has this incident taught you about how you manage stress?	*I don't admit to feeling stressed and take it out on my family and colleagues.*
What has this incident taught you about how you look after your well-being?	*That it is okay to admit feeling stressed and ask for help from people I trust.*

Working with persons with difficult or distressing stories, suicidal thoughts, feelings of extreme hopelessness and/or self-harming behaviour means being exposed to a range of intense and extreme emotions. These predominantly include anxiety, sadness, guilt and a sense of responsibility for both the person and the worker (Briggs, 2008). As discussed in chapters 5 and 6, some workers may experience certain behaviours of clients as extremely stressful. For example, when a client has cut or burned himself/herself, it may arouse for the worker a range of feelings including extreme shock, anger, fear, panic, all of which can be hard to bear. Similarly, listening to a client expressing suicidal thoughts or hearing about a client who died by suicide can also be emotionally challenging and stressful for the worker, as captured in the case scenarios below.

CASE SCENARIO 7.3

Paul, an experienced prison officer, often recalls his first week, many years ago, working in a youth remand centre, and the shock of witnessing a young lad Peter who hit his head against a glass door. After first aid was carried out by a staff member, Paul and another staff member took Peter to the local Emergency Department, wherein he received suturing for a large deep cut over his right eye. A few days later, Paul remembered his disbelief and frustration on seeing Peter pull at the sutures over his eye. At that time, Paul struggled to understand Peter's behaviour and felt so angry towards him. Later that day, he found it helpful to talk about the incident and his feelings with a colleague.

CASE SCENARIO 7.4

Maya, a community mental health nurse, appreciated having a space to talk with her clinical supervisor about the impact of working with a client who wished to end her life. Maya presented Torie, a mother of two young children whom she had established a good therapeutic relationship. Maya discussed how she struggled to understand why Torie wanted to die especially as she had so much going for her – two daughters aged five and three years old and a supportive partner and family. Maya was concerned that she felt frustrated with Torie and as a result she found it difficult to demonstrate compassion and empathy. During the supervision session, the supervisor facilitated Maya to examine her beliefs and values about suicide and discuss how they might affect her interventions and working relationship with Torie. Having the opportunity to reflect on her beliefs about suicide helped Maya to have a better understanding of her responses and how they had impacted on her work with suicidal clients in general, and in particular with Torie. With time and self-reflection, Maya learnt to develop a greater understanding of Torie's suicidal thoughts.

CASE SCENARIO 7.5

Andrew, an approved Social Worker, remembered the first time he lost a client by suicide. His name was Tom, a 75-year-old widower, whom he had worked closely with following a diagnosis of early onset of Dementia. Andrew developed a very good rapport with Tom and they both enjoyed talking about their favourite sport rugby. A year after his discharge, Andrew was saddened to hear that Tom had hung himself. Several years later, Andrew remembered Tom fondly and his wealth of knowledge and passion for rugby.

REFLECTIVE QUESTIONS

1. Which of the above scenarios do you consider the most challenging and for what reason?
2. Which of the above scenarios do you consider the least challenging and for what reason?
3. Identify a similar experience in your capacity of helping that caused you to feel sad/frustrated, angry towards a client/person whom you were helping?
4. What was the incident(s)?
5. How did you respond at the time?
6. Reflecting back, how helpful or not was your response?
7. What strategies did you use to look after yourself at that time and afterwards?
8. How might you respond to a similar incident in the future?
9. What did you learn about yourself from this incident?

Emotional labour

Helping someone has to include an emotional element (Mc Queen, 2004). While caring 'for' someone is usually associated with the performance of a task or tasks, caring 'about' someone refers to the feelings that are explicitly in the working relationship and resulting care (Stickley & Freshwater, 2002). Establishing, sustaining and ending relationships with clients require hard work, compassion, commitment and energy from the worker. Workers whose everyday work involves caring about and working with a person who is expressing suicidal thoughts and/or exhibiting self-harming behaviours involves what is described as emotional labour (Hochschild, 1983).

Emotional labour, first identified by Hochschild (1983), refers to the management of emotions in the performance of everyday work. Based on the study of flight attendants, Hochschild (1983) conceptualised emotional labour as an underreported, undervalued, invisible component of service sector 'people' work, largely undertaken by women. A more recent definition describes it as an effort involved when workers 'regulate their emotional display in an attempt to meet organizationally based expectations specific to their roles' (Brotheridge & Lee, 2003: 365). Emotional labour can be performed through either 'surface' or 'deep' acting (Hochschild, 1983). Surface acting involves 'managing the expression of behaviour rather than feelings' (Williams, 2003: 516); deep acting, on the other hand, involves the actor attempting to actually experience or feel the emotion that he/she wishes or is expected to display. Employment that involves emotional labour includes workers such as nurses, social workers or first responders, whose role involve face-to-face contact with members of the public and require the worker to maintain a certain distance, as well as produce an emotional state in another person (Hochschild, 1983). As such, emotional labour is a strategy that allows workers to manage emotions and sustain an outward appearance that produces in others a sense of being cared for in a friendly and safe place (Smith & Gray, 2000, 2001).

Compassion fatigue

According to Figley (1995: 1), 'there is a cost to caring'; workers who are exposed to the stories of clients' distress, fears and suffering may experience similar feelings because they care'. In fact, Figley (2002: 1434) argues that 'the very act of being compassionate and empathetic extracts a cost under most circumstances'. In the field of helping, workers commonly experience 'compassion fatigue' (Figley, 2002) due to the emotional labour that is often part of the therapeutic or helping work (Mann, 2005; Tehrani, 2007). Identified by Figley (1995), compassion fatigue, also known as secondary traumatic stress (STS), is a common outcome of providing therapy/care and/or help, which until recently was unrecognised as an occupational hazard of professional helping and as a result received minimal attention (Everall & Paulson, 2004). Workers who work with people who have experienced traumatic events may suffer from compassion fatigue, which is a stress-related syndrome that results from the cumulative emotional drain on the worker's capacity to care for others, and is the direct result of working with people who present emotional challenges to workers (Figley, 1995), including clients who have experienced suicidal and self-harming behaviour.

Working in the high-touch professions or helping occupations can be positive; however, the intensity and scope of human distress that workers might face and moreover the most traumatic incident such as the suicide of a client should not be underemphasised. Skovholt and Trotter-Mathison (2011) identify specific characteristics of professionals/helpers and/or components of helping that make workers in the field of helping more susceptible to compassion fatigue or burnout; these include listening to emotionally shocking and distressing material along with the use of the skill of empathy. According to Larson (1993: 30), these skills could be considered as 'a double-edged sword'; that is, while they are simultaneously the worker's/helper's greatest asset, implementing such skills on a regular basis exposes the worker to real vulnerability. As Figley (1995) points out, it is not simply the acute sense of empathy that counsellors/workers/helpers possess, but it is the fact that being empathic exposes the workers to the struggles and sufferings of the person in front of them, which can have an impact on them. For workers, the excessive level of occupational stress may also result from working closely with clients over a long period of time as well as higher levels of helplessness and a feeling of being isolated from a support network (Figley, 1995).

Burnout

The term 'burnout', first coined by Freudenberger (1974), refers to occupationally related negative psychological problems. Although work-related, burnout is not caused by one single factor; several factors including individual, interpersonal and organisational factors are known to contribute to it. One of the components of burnout is emotional exhaustion, and relationships have been found between this and emotional labour. Burnout does not happen suddenly; it is an ongoing process that begins slowly and progresses through several developmental stages. Workers in the helping and related fields are prone to burnout, as a result of the emotional strain of working with others who are troubled over a long period of time (Maslach, 1982). According to Christine Maslach (1982), who has written extensively on the topic and developed the well-known research instrument – The Maslach Burnout Inventory (MBI) (Maslach & Jackson, 1981) – burnout is a phenomenon of extreme physical, mental and emotional exhaustion, decreased work motivation, depersonalisation and the perception of diminished professional achievements. For the worker, depersonalisation may be manifested by a lack of empathy towards others and as such detached relationships with clients and colleagues, together with a withdrawal from any active efforts to meet the needs of others. Although burnout and compassion fatigue may cause the worker to experience similar feelings, a key difference between them relates to the cause of the symptoms; as described above, compassion fatigue is the direct result of hearing emotionally shocking stories or material from clients; in contrast, burnout can result from working with any client group (Everall & Paulson, 2004).

REFLECTIVE EXERCISE

Consider the definitions of emotional labour, compassion fatigue and burnout and answer the following questions.

1. As a worker/helper, how do you manage emotions and sustain an outward appearance that produces in others a sense of being cared for in a friendly and safe place? Illustrate your answer with examples.
2. As a worker/helper, how have you managed the intensity and scope of human distress such as the death of a client by suicide? Illustrate your answer with examples.
3. As a worker/helper, how might you be prone to burnout, as a result of the emotional strain of working with suicidal clients and/or clients who self-harm over a long period of time? Illustrate your answer with examples.

Impact of stress on the worker and organisation

Although defined differently, the impact of compassion fatigue and burnout on the worker which are both cumulative (Skovholt & Trotter-Mathison, 2011) may result in a range of physical, psychological and/or social problems. Workers, who work with people who are expressing suicidal behaviour or who self-harm, may experience a range of symptoms such as insomnia, lack of energy, poor concentration, heightened emotions such as anger, grief or anxiety, reduced self-esteem, disrupted personal relationships and decreased job satisfaction. At the outset, the effects of 'caring' may have a more subtle impact on the worker, yet the longer the worker is in distress and particularly in the absence of formal supportive systems, the more likely that the problems will escalate and be noticed by others, although at times such symptoms of stress may not always be visible or identifiable. In the work context, co-workers may over time begin to see signs of fatigue, boredom, negativity, disinterest in work and/or a decreased ability to complete tasks. In addition, clients or those being helped may also be aware of their workers' disinterest or negativity. However, they may not feel that they are in a position to say anything for fear of upsetting the worker or the likelihood of possible repercussions. Failure to address or resolve such problems may result in more severe impairments for the worker, including feelings of helplessness and a sense of feeling stuck or trapped that may manifest in negative attitudes towards self, co-workers, work and life itself (Skovholt & Trotter-Mathison, 2011). Notwithstanding the impact of compassion fatigue or burnout on the worker's quality of life, a high level of stress is also likely to impinge on the worker's ability to make decisions and/or establish and sustain strong relationships with clients and/or users of the service. These behaviours are the warning signs of the worker failing to engage in the helping process, which in turn is likely to reduce the quality and efficacy of the care/help provided and as such have a negative effect for co-workers and the organisation.

Working with distressed and traumatised people in whatever role is challenging and it therefore seems reasonable that strategies are implemented to counteract the effects of stress, compassion fatigue or burnout. However, for many workers outside of psychotherapeutic settings, there is minimal, if any, formal support strategies such as clinical supervision, for identifying and processing their responses and feelings (Turp, 2003). With little or no support systems available, practitioners and workers are likely to have difficulty in offering emotional and psychological support and/or in feeling contained themselves when working with people who present with suicidal and self-harming behaviours. Given that the effectiveness of helpers depends on their own health and well-being, caring for self while caring for others is therefore a priority for all helpers.

REFLECTIVE EXERCISE

Reflect on a time wherein you were working with a client who self-harmed and you felt stressed. Answer the following questions, illustrating your answer with examples.

1. How did you know that you were 'stressed'?
2. What physical symptoms did you experience?
3. How would you describe your mood?
4. What were your thoughts at the time?
5. What other words (if any) did you use to describe how you felt?
6. What things did you do less of at the time, for example socialising with family or friends?
7. What things did you do more of at the time, for example lying in bed during the day?

8. Did any of your co-workers notice that you were stressed, if so, what did they notice?
9. Did any of your family/friends notice that you were stressed, if so, what did they notice?
10. Who did you talk to about how you were feeling?
11. Who did you not talk to about how you were feeling and for what reasons?
12. Identify 1–2 'warning signs' which might alert you to being more aware of your stress in the future, for example disturbed sleep, irritable mood.

Using self-care strategies in work

As stated at the outset of the chapter, self-care is an ongoing preventative activity. Implementing self-care in work involves not only changes in behaviour but also changes in beliefs about oneself. Self-care must be grounded in a sense of self-worth and the conscious or unconscious understanding that the person/worker is deserving of care and that it is right and appropriate that one should be treated with proper care and respect (Turp, 2003). The worker has the right to exercise the function of self-care for himself/herself and that it is not reserved for the organisation or manager alone.

Beliefs about self-care

In order to develop the capacity for self-care, it is important that the worker is aware of his/her beliefs and assumptions about self-care and how such beliefs can either enhance our working lives or add stress as reflected in the examples shown in Table 7.1.

Table 7.1 Beliefs about self-care

Enhance self-care	Inhibit self-care
I deserve to care for myself and others	Other people's needs come before mine
It is okay to ask for help	Asking for help is a sign of weakness
I am responsible for myself and my work	I am responsible for others and everything
I cannot 'fix' the client's problems but I can help the person to find his/her own solutions	I need to 'fix it' for the client and the family and/or the organisation
I can say no when needed and so can others say no to me	I find it difficult to say no
I am aware of my own limits	I should be able to do everything
I endeavour to respect my work and personal time equally	I let work interfere with my personal time
I endeavour to respect others' need for personal time and work equally	I don't respect others' need for personal time and work

REFLECTIVE EXERCISE

Identify two beliefs about self-care that you can relate to as a worker. Illustrate your answer with examples.	I.
	2.
How do these beliefs enhance and/or inhibit your self-care?	I.
	2.

The following fictitious case scenario illustrates the impact of stress on a worker.

CASE SCENARIO 7.6

Ruby worked as a teacher in a large Comprehensive school. Students liked her and often approached her to talk about various 'issues'. Although Ruby enjoyed her relationship with the students, she was increasingly aware that she felt emotionally tired and stressed. Her work colleague and friend Jade suggested that she speak to their Principal, who was known to be very supportive, and ask for some time off. Ruby considered Jade's suggestion; however, she decided not to ask for help, believing that the Principal might think that 'she wasn't a good teacher'. Instead Ruby continued her work and increasingly felt disinterested in her job. Several months later, she was signed off work with high blood pressure.

REFLECTIVE QUESTIONS

1. Identify three possible reasons why Ruby decided not to ask for help?
2. What might hinder you asking for help in your area of work?
3. What would you do in a similar incident and why?

Self-care strategies and principles

The following section presents various self-caring strategies and principles for the worker to develop, implement and sustain. These are by no means intended to be a definitive or exhaustive list. Since there is no a universal method for implementing self-care (Norcross, 2000), each worker will need different self-care strategies at different stages of their career and it is important to devise your own strategies to cope with the stresses associated with being part of an organisation. The practice exercise in Table 7.2 can be used to develop self-care strategies and principles to meet your personal needs.

Table 7.2 Developing self-care strategies and principles

Self-monitoring strategies

Identify your beliefs and assumptions about self-care.	Example: 'It's great if you have the time, but I am always busy'.
Be aware of your defeating internal dialogue.	Example: 'I can't say no'; 'I shouldn't be upset'; 'I should always be strong'; 'Other people's needs are more important than mine'.
Be mindful of self-neglecting behaviours.	Example: Feeling overworked and stressed, yet not refusing when asked to do more work.
Acknowledge the potential hazards of the helping endeavour on your health and well-being.	Example: 'I use to take work home and worry about clients, which was not good for my physical and mental health'; 'I now go for a short walk after work to clear my mind of all the stresses'.
Recognise how you are affected by stress – physically, emotionally, cognitively and behaviourally.	Example: 'When I am stressed, I feel nauseous, tearful, find it difficult to concentrate and withdraw from people'.
Monitor how stress impacts on your interpersonal relationships with clients, work colleagues, family and friends.	Example: 'I know I can be very irritable and impatient with everyone, when I am stressed'.
Give yourself permission to have self-care needs.	Example: 'It's important for my well-being to take care of my physical and mental health'.
Be mindful that self-monitoring is a continuous ethical responsibility for all helpers and workers.	Example: 'I have a responsibility to myself and others to take care of my physical and mental health'.

Taking Action

Internalise beliefs about the importance of self-care.	Example: 'I believe it is important to take care of my physical and mental health, that is why I do not work take on certain extra things at work'.
Identify and state needs clearly and succinctly.	Example: 'I need support and guidance when working with suicidal clients'; 'I find it difficult to work with you when you dismiss the client's cutting as attention seeking'.
Ask for assistance, support and guidance when needed.	Example: 'What should I say when the client tells me, he wants to die?'; 'How should I respond to the client when she shows me her scars from cutting?'
Maintain boundaries and find the right level of attachment with the helpee.	Example: Working professionally, not getting over/under involved with client.
Learn to know when to expend energy and when to preserve energy.	Example: Be mindful about what things you expend and preserve energy.
Say no clearly and succinctly.	Example: 'No, I can't let you have your blades now'.

continued overleaf

Table 7.2 *continued*

Avail of formal and informal support strategies, for example clinical supervision, support group, colleagues and manager.	Example: *Use and encourage the value of formal and informal support strategies in your area of work.*
Talk about feelings with colleagues.	Example: *Give yourself permission to talk about feelings with colleagues.*
Promote a work culture that fosters self-care for all clients and workers within the organisation.	Example: *Acknowledge and encourage the importance of self-care for all clients and workers within the organisation.*
Apply stress management strategies as an ongoing preventative practice.	Example: *Regular exercise; swimming; running.*
Support and encourage colleagues and co-workers' capacity to self-care.	Example: *Support and encourage colleagues and co-workers' capacity to self-care.*
Act as a role model of valuing and placing importance on caring for self.	Example: *Model the importance on caring for self, leaving work on time.*

The following case scenarios illustrate how different self-care strategies were implemented in different work settings.

CASE SCENARIO 7.7

Joy works as a support worker in a residential home for adolescents. Although challenging, she likes her job and enjoys working with young people; she also feels very lucky to work with caring and supportive colleagues. Over the last six months, there have been rumours about proposed changes to the structure of residential care in Social Services. 'Another reorganisation' and the possibility of redundancy have prompted staff to feel anxious about their future and their careers. This together with the recent death by suicide of a former client led Joy to feeling very tense, irritable and powerless. Recognising the impact of her emotions on her well-being and her relationships both at work and at home; she decided to discuss her responses with Tom, the team leader, whom she respects and finds very supportive and non-judgemental. Following discussion with Tom and having the opportunity to consider what short-term self-care strategies might be helpful at this point, she decided to take two weeks annual leave. Joy also decided that on her return from leave she would re-join the monthly staff support group, which she had stopped attending due to staff shortages.

CASE SCENARIO 7.8

James works as a school counsellor in a large Comprehensive School; part of his job involves supporting and assisting teachers when working with clients who are expressing suicidal thoughts or self-harming behaviours. As an experienced counsellor, he is aware of the importance of good self-care as well as his ethical responsibility to ensure that he looks after his own well-being so that he can work safely and effectively with his clients and colleagues. Although he utilises the formal support systems available to him (e.g. clinical supervision), he is mindful that he needs to manage his work/home boundaries much better, as he is aware that he is spending little time with his two young daughters. Having given this thought, James has promised himself and his partner that he will leave work on time and not check his emails after 7pm each evening.

REFLECTIVE QUESTIONS

1. Have the above examples shown good self-care strategies or not?
2. If you were Joy, what would you do in a similar incident and why?
3. How do you manage your work/home boundaries?

Conclusion

Caring for self is essential for effective, competent and safe work, as well as for establishing and maintaining good working and personal relationships. However, learning to care for self in the workplace is a challenging, life-long, purposeful, personal and professional activity. Because, self-care is often compromised, it is therefore important to be constantly mindful of its importance and value. For the worker, it requires a shift in thinking and behaving and an openness to identify self-neglecting tendencies in order to enhance the capacity to self-care. As with most learning, acquiring skills and developing the confidence to implement self-care strategies requires time, practice and support from co-workers, managers and the organisation.

REFLECTIVE QUESTIONS

1. In your own words, how would you explain the concept of self-care to a colleague?
2. What do you think are the benefits of self-care for the worker, client/user, co-workers and the organisation?
3. Identify three factors that might prevent workers from using self-care strategies in practice.
4. Identify three things that you might do during the next month to improve your self-care in work.

REFERENCES

Barnett, J.E., Johnston, L.C. and Hillard, D. (2006) Psychological wellness as an ethical imperative. In VandeCreek, L. and Allen, J.B. (eds.) *Innovations in Clinical Practice: Focus on Health and Wellness*. Sarasota, FL: Professional Resources Press, pp 257–271.

Briggs, S. (2008) Postvention: The impact of suicide and suicidal behaviour on family members, professionals and organisations. In Briggs, S., Lemma, A. and Crouch, W. (eds.) *Relating to*

Self-Harm and Suicide, Psychoanalytic Perspectives on Practice, Theory and Prevention, London: Routledge, pp 224–237.

Brotheridge, C.M. and Lee, R. (2003) Development and validation of the Emotional Labour Scale. *Journal of Occupational and Organisational Labour*, 76: 365–379.

Corey, M.S. and Corey, G. (2011) *Becoming a Helper*. 6th ed. Belmont, CA: Brookes Cole.

Department of Health. (DH) (2010) *The NHS Outcomes Framework for 2011/2012*. London: DH.

Department of Health. (DH) (2012) Health and Social Care Bill. Retrieved from http://healthandcare.dh.gov.uk/category/health-and-social-care-bill/ on 16 August 2013.

Everall, R.D. and Paulson, B.L. (2004) Burnout and secondary traumatic stress: Impact on ethical behaviour. *Canadian Journal of Counselling*, 38(1): 25–35.

Figley, C.R. (1995) Compassion fatigue: Toward a new understanding of the costs of caring. In Stamm, B.H. (ed.) *Secondary Trauma Stress: Self-Care Issues for Clinicians, Researchers and Educators*. Lutherville, MD: Sidran Press, pp 3–28.

Figley, C.R. (2002) Compassion fatigue: Psychotherapists' chronic lack of self-care. *Journal of Clinical Psychology*, 58: 1433–1441.

Freudenberger, H. (1974) Staff burnout. *Journal of Social Work*, 30: 159–165.

Hochschild, A.R. (1983) *The Managed Heart: Commercialization of Human Feeling*. Berkley, CA: University of California Press.

Larson, D.G. (1993) *The Helper's Journey*. Champaign, IL: Research Press.

Mann, S. (2005) A health care model of emotional labour. *Journal of Health Organisational and Management*, 9(4–5): 304–317.

Maslach, C. (1982) *Burnout: The Cost of Caring*. Cambridge. Malor Books.

Maslach, C. and Jackson, S.E. (1981) *The Maslach Burnout Inventory*. Palo Alto, CA: Consulting Psychologists Press.

Mc Queen, A. (2004) Emotional intelligence in nursing work. *Journal of Advanced Nursing*, 47(1): 101–108.

Norcross, J.C. (2000) Psychotherapist self-care: Practitioner-tested, research-informed strategies. *Professional Psychology: Research and Practice*, 31: 710–7143.

Norcross, J.C. and Guy, J.D. (2007) *Learning to Leave It at the Office: A Guide to Psychotherapist Self-Care*. New York: Guilford Press.

Reeves, A. (2010) *Counselling Suicidal Clients*. London: Sage.

Skovholt, T.M. and Trotter-Mathison, M. (2011) *The Resilient Practitioner Burnout Prevention and Self-Care Strategies for Counselors, Therapists, Teachers and Health Professionals*. 2nd ed. London: Routledge.

Smith, P. (1992) *The Emotional Labour of Nursing*. London: Macmillan.

Smith, P. and Gray, B. (2000) *The Emotional Labour of Nursing: How Student and Qualified Nurses Learn to Care*. London: South Bank University.

Smith, P. and Gray, B. (2001) Reassessing the concept of emotional labour in student nurse education: Role of link lecturers and mentors in a time of change. *Nurse Education Today*, 21: 230–237.

Stickley, T. and Freshwater, D. (2002) The art of loving and the therapeutic relationship. *Nursing Inquiry*, 6(4): 250–256.

Tehrani, N. (2007) The cost of caring-the impact of secondary trauma on assumptions, values and beliefs. *Counselling Psychology Quarterly*, 20(4): 325–339.

Turp, M. (2003) *Hidden Self-Harm Narratives from Psychotherapy*. London: Jessica Kingsley.

Williams, C. (2003) Sky service: The demands of emotional labour in the airline industry. *Gender, Work and Organisation*, 10: 513–548.

CHAPTER 8

Suicide and Self-Harm Prevention and Reduction

Louise Doyle

Introduction

Preventing and reducing suicide and self-harm is an important public health target for most countries in the developed and increasingly in the developing world. This is particularly so in light of the projected 1.5 million annual deaths by suicide by 2020 (Hadlaczky et al., 2011). This chapter will look at national and international prevention initiatives that are in place to reduce suicide and self-harm. Specific suicide and where available self-harm prevention initiatives will be examined and the challenges of implementation of such initiatives will be considered. This chapter will include a consideration of both the general population approach to suicide and self-harm prevention and also the targeted approach incorporating specific 'at risk' groups. The focus of this chapter is largely on suicide prevention as most of the research and policy literature is heavily focused towards prevention of attempted and completed suicide. However, as discussed in chapters 3 and 4, most of the risk factors for suicide overlap with those of self-harm. Therefore, many of the initiatives detailed below will have some utility in preventing not just completed suicide but also self-harm on a broad level. Towards the end of this chapter, there is a brief consideration of some harm reduction approaches which are specific to those who already engage in self-harm (without suicidal intent) and which are viewed as a move away from prevention towards a more effective and supportive intervention for those who self-harm (Inckle, 2011). Attention is also paid to the growth of support and self-help through the Internet, which can provide information and support to those who engage in repetitive self-harm.

LEARNING OUTCOMES

By the end of this chapter, you should be better able to:

1. identify general population approaches to prevention of suicide and self-harm;
2. identify targeted approaches to prevention of suicide and self-harm;

3. discuss some of the challenges inherent in suicide and self-harm prevention;
4. identify harm reduction and alternative coping and support strategies for those who engage in self-harm.

The World Health Organisation (WHO) and the International Association for Suicide Prevention (IASP) both advocate a broad-based approach to suicide prevention. Within this approach, suicide prevention strategies are twofold and complementary and take the form of focusing on general population (universal) approaches and targeted approaches which focus on high-risk individuals or groups. The European Commission and the World Health Organisation have together developed the 'European Pact for Mental Health and Well-Being' which was adopted by the 27 European Union (EU) member states (European Commission and World Health Organisation, 2008). The first of five priority areas identified in this pact is that of 'prevention of depression and suicide', recognising that every nine minutes a citizen dies by suicide in the EU. Within this priority area, five key actions are identified:

1. improve the training of health professionals and key actors within the social sector on mental health;
2. restrict access to potential means for suicide;
3. take measures to raise mental health awareness in the general public, among health professionals and other relevant sectors;
4. take measures to reduce risk factors for suicide such as excessive drinking, drug use and social exclusion, depression and stress;
5. provide support mechanisms after suicide attempts, such as emotional support helplines for those bereaved by suicide.

It is evident from reviewing these high-priority areas that they span across both general population approaches and targeted approaches to suicide prevention. The next section of this chapter will focus on identifying in more depth some common general population and targeted approaches to suicide prevention. It should be noted however that this is not an exhaustive list of global suicide prevention initiatives.

General population approaches

The aim of a general population approach to suicide prevention is to promote positive mental health and well-being and strengthen coping and problem-solving skills in the general population. In addition, general population approaches work to increase the availability and access to support services, decrease stigma and in turn increase help-seeking. A review of a number of national suicide prevention policies has identified a number of common general population approaches to suicide prevention. Some commonly identified general population approaches include the following:

School-based initiatives

Suicidal behaviour and self-harm often emerge in adolescence. School provides an opportunistic setting to reach out to large numbers of young people and is a prime location for mental health promotion initiatives which could ultimately improve formal help-seeking and reduce self-harm and suicidal behaviour. Chapter 10 identifies some specific ways in which schools and individual school staff can best respond to and prevent self-harm and suicidal behaviour. In addition, there is a large number of school-based suicide prevention/mental health promotion programmes and while beneficial effects have been demonstrated (Lake & Gould, 2011), evidence from evaluations of early school-based initiatives focusing on suicide, in particular, suggest the need for caution as some programmes were found to have iatrogenic effects – adverse effects caused by the programme itself (Shaffer et al., 1991). In light of this, it is essential that programmes introduced to the school setting are evidence-based and continually evaluated.

School-based screening programmes have been shown to identify those 'at-risk' young people and to link them in to appropriate mental health services prior to a suicidal crisis emerging (Lake & Gould, 2011). These young people may not have been identified in the absence of screening. However, there are a number of difficulties with school-based screening programmes. They work on the premise that schools have a relationship with local mental health providers and that there is adequate mental health services to refer an at-risk student; however, this is not always the case. In some countries, Child and Adolescent Mental Health Services (CAMHS) are over-stretched and have significant waiting lists meaning that many adolescents may be identified as potentially 'at-risk' but the services are not adequate to respond to them. In addition, screening programmes by their nature yield a large number of false positive results thereby placing a significant burden on schools and the mental health providers.

Another school-based strategy is the use of educational and skills-based programmes to increase awareness of mental health issues and knowledge of how and where to seek help if required. These awareness programmes have moved away from a sole focus on 'suicide' and instead have broadened out to include the wider issues of mental health and help-seeking and aim to prevent suicidal behaviour through the promotion of coping strategies and problem-solving. The small group method of delivering many of these programmes may also play a role in enhancing social affiliations and potentially social connectedness (Lake & Gould, 2011).

A strategy focusing on friends of those who experience suicidal behaviour and in particular self-harm is another initiative that warrants attention. Research indicates that if an adolescent engages in self-harm or suicidal behaviour, they are most likely to seek help from a friend rather than a formal help source (Morey et al., 2008). However, it is likely that friends are not adequately prepared for that role and do not have the necessary skills, knowledge or indeed the psychological resources to respond appropriately to a friend experiencing self-harm or suicidal behaviour. There is therefore a requirement that adolescents have some knowledge about how to respond in such a situation and how to refer on to an appropriate adult. This ideally should form part of a mental health promotion programme. One such programme, 'The Signs of Self-Injury Program' has shown some promising results in a pilot study in the United States (Muehlenkamp et al., 2010). Results suggest that having completed the programme, participants displayed significant improvements in accurate knowledge and attitudes about self-harm as well as a significant increase in the 'helping desire' attitude indicating that adolescents were more open to helping a friend who was self-harming (Muehlenkamp et al., 2010). In light of the fact that an act of self-harm is more likely disclosed to a friend more than any other person, including information in a mental health promotion programme about responding appropriately to a friend's self-harm would seem appropriate.

Public awareness and reducing stigma

The development and roll-out of public education and awareness campaigns is a key feature in many national suicide prevention policies and is recommended by the World Health Organisation (WHO, 2012). These campaigns largely focus on increasing awareness of mental health problems and suicide and increasing knowledge about how and where to seek help if distressed. Another significant component of these initiatives focuses on reducing stigma, as it recognised that stigma attached to mental health difficulties and suicidal behaviour is one of the biggest challenges to prevention. Awareness campaigns may take the form of billboards, radio, TV and cinema infomercials which are sometimes targeted at specific groups (e.g. adolescents and young adults). They also involve delivery of short workshops or educational programmes developed and delivered at a national level or alternatively on a local level by community groups. A review of international public awareness campaigns which focused on depression and suicide found that such programmes improve the general publics' knowledge about depression and suicide and make a moderate contribution to a decrease in stigma and better social acceptance of people with mental health difficulties (Dumesnil & Verger, 2009). Programmes which were more focused and sustained and which employed different methods of message dissemination appeared to be more successful. However, it was not possible to determine if these programmes increased help-seeking or reduced suicidal behaviour.

There is an important distinction to be drawn between de-stigmatising suicidal behaviour and de-stigmatising the person who engages in suicidal behaviour. It has been identified that becoming more accepting of suicidal thoughts and behaviours in a public campaign is a risky proposition (Pearson, 2011). In showing sensitivity when discussing suicide, it is possible that the act of suicide is legitimised, albeit implicitly and unintentionally. There is therefore a fine balance to be achieved between de-stigmatising mental health problems and the individuals who experience them, while concomitantly ensuring that the public message is not that suicide is an inevitable solution to significant distress.

Restricting access to means of suicide

Restricting access to means of suicide falls within the remit of both a general population approach in that it is broadly based and a targeted approach as the intention is to reduce the risk of suicide in those who are distressed and vulnerable. Reducing access to means of suicide has been recognised by the WHO as one of the primary suicide prevention strategies and accordingly it features in almost all suicide prevention strategies throughout the world (Yip et al., 2012). When someone is experiencing a suicidal crisis, having access to means of self-harm makes it more likely that suicide will occur. In addition, impulsivity is a known risk factor for suicidal behaviour and once again impulsive behaviour combined with easy access to means of suicide is more likely to result in an outcome of completed suicide. If access to lethal methods is restricted, there is the potential that suicidal impulses will pass without a suicidal act taking place. The following are methods of suicide and actions taken to reduce means to them:

- *Suicide by poisoning:* Suicide and self-harm by poisoning is perhaps one of the methods most amenable to reduction by restricting access to means. This method of suicidal behaviour is common amongst females in the United Kingdom and Ireland, and self-poisoning using analgesics such as paracetamol has been a particular cause for concern considering the relative ease of availability and the medical seriousness of overdose with paracetamol. Legislation to restrict the sale of paracetamol was introduced in the United Kingdom in 1998 and in Ireland in 2001 and both countries have seen a reduction in overdoses of paracetamol and products containing paracetamol since the introduction of controls (Corcoran et al., 2010; Hawton et al., 2012). Self-poisoning using paracetamol does however remain a cause for concern.
- *Suicide by jumping from a height:* Restricting access to tall buildings or elevated places (cliffs, bridges etc.) is difficult in view of the relatively high number of these places in both cities (tall buildings, bridges) and more rural areas (cliffs). While a number of practical measures such as monitoring access to the roofs of tall buildings can be implemented, the relative ease of access and high lethality means that it remains a particular problem. Gunnell et al. (2005a) have identified a number of strategies in place in areas where suicide by jumping is common (The Golden Gate Bridge in San Francisco, Beachy Head in the UK). Interventions include monitored surveillance cameras, regular patrols of the area, freephone telephone lines to suicide prevention organisations and notices offering contact details for potential sources of help.
- *Suicide by hanging:* Suicide by hanging is a common method of suicide in many countries, including the United Kingdom and Ireland. The easy availability of ligature points in a range of settings means that preventing/reducing access to this method of suicide is generally not possible. In recognition of this, it is suggested that strategies to reduce suicide by hanging should focus on the prevention of suicide in controlled

environments (e.g. prisons, psychiatric hospitals), the emergency management of near-hanging, and on the primary prevention of suicide in general (Gunnell et al., 2005b).

- *Suicide by firearms:* Suicide using firearms is particularly common in those countries where guns are widely available (e.g. US) and less common where guns are more difficult to obtain. However, even within these countries, suicide by firearms is more common in rural areas where firearms may be legally held for agricultural reasons. Reducing suicide by firearm centres largely on tightening of restrictions relating to legal gun ownership.

- *Pesticide poisoning:* Suicide by pesticide poisoning is uncommon in Western society; however, it is very common in developing countries where it is carried out predominantly by young women (Chen et al., 2011), and approximately one-third of worldwide suicides are as a result of pesticide poisoning. Once again, this is a very accessible method of self-harm, particularly in rural areas, and is highly fatal. Research on pesticide poisoning has shown that it is more common in people without a history of mental health difficulties and is more likely to be an impulsive reaction to a family quarrel. A number of ways have been identified to reduce suicide by pesticide poisoning including developing secure storage policies which restrict access to a licensed owner and the development of less toxic alternatives to pesticides.

- *Charcoal burning:* The phenomenon of burning charcoal to create a toxic and fatal level of carbon monoxide has gained prominence in Asia over recent decades. This method accounted for one-fifth of suicides in Hong Kong between 2007 and 2009 and almost one-third in Taiwan between 2008 and 2010 (Chen et al., 2013). This increase is largely attributed to the media portrayal of it being a relatively painless, calm and non-violent death (Chen et al., 2011). There is evidence to suggest that this method of suicide has attracted a cohort of individuals who would not traditionally have considered suicide as an option, as their sociodemographic and clinical characteristics are different from those who complete suicide using other means (Chen et al., 2013). It appears to be particularly prominent in economically active middle-aged men who are experiencing financial distress. A recent initiative in Hong Kong which removed charcoal from shop shelves and required individuals to ask an assistant to obtain charcoal for purchase appears to have reduced the number of local suicides (Yip et al., 2010). Although suicide through charcoal burning is not currently a common method of suicide in Western societies, there is the potential for it to become one due to the amount and type of information about this method of suicide freely available on the Internet (Chen et al., 2013).

Two other methods of suicide, domestic gas poisoning and motor vehicle exhaust gas suicide, have also been impacted by a reduction in access to these means. The installation of catalytic convertors in cars has resulted in a dramatic decrease in the number of suicides associated with motor vehicle exhaust gas. Similarly, a significant reduction in the amount of carbon monoxide in domestic gas supplies corresponded with a steady decrease in suicide rates in a number of countries including the United Kingdom. Both are salient examples of how a reduction in overall suicide rates can be achieved by reducing access to lethal means of suicide.

Reducing harmful use of alcohol

Alcohol misuse is significantly linked to self-harm and completed suicide. Restricting the availability of alcohol to reduce the harmful use of alcohol is particularly critical within populations with a high prevalence of alcohol use (WHO, 2012). A WHO global strategy to reduce the harmful effects of alcohol has identified a number of different ways that a reduction in alcohol use might be achieved, including initiatives focusing on marketing and pricing policy (WHO, 2010). However, there has been resistance in some quarters, particularly the drinks industry, with regard to many of these strategies which will ultimately result in reduced revenue for those involved in the drinks industry.

Responsible media reporting of suicide

The manner in which suicidal acts are reported or portrayed in the media can have a negative impact and facilitate imitative suicidal behaviour or 'copycat' suicides in those people exposed to such reporting (Machlin et al., 2013). It has been identified that suicide rates may rise after media reporting of suicide, especially if it is given prominence, if the methods are reported in detail, if the suicide is glamorised or if it involves a celebrity (Chapple et al., 2013). Consequently the WHO recommends that the media:

- avoid language which sensationalises or normalises suicide or presents it as a solution to a problem;
- avoid pictures and explicit details of the method used;
- provide information about where to seek help. (WHO, 2012)

Targeted approaches

Targeted approaches to suicide and self-harm prevention are those which aim to reduce the risk of suicidal behaviour among high-risk groups and vulnerable people. Some common targeted approaches evident in national suicide prevention policies include the following:

Training gatekeepers

Gatekeepers are those people who come into regular contact with the general public on account of their professional status. As gatekeepers interact with the general public in a variety of settings, they can be trained to recognise risk factors and warning signs of suicidal behaviour (WHO, 2012). Gatekeepers in this context comprise health care staff including those in primary healthcare, emergency departments and mental health services. Other gatekeepers include prison officers, teachers, community leaders, police and religious leaders. Many gatekeepers are in regular contact with people who are at a high risk for suicidal behaviour, hence the potential here for suicide prevention initiatives.

A number of training programmes have been developed to help gatekeepers become better skilled at interacting with people experiencing a suicidal crisis. As identified in chapter 6, one such programme is ASIST (Applied Suicide Intervention Skills Training) which is a two-day interactive workshop on suicide first aid. This programme is designed for both professionals and the general public, and the aim is to help caregivers/gatekeepers provide emergency first aid to people at risk of suicidal behaviour. During the workshop, participants examine their attitudes to suicide, learn how to recognise and review the risk of suicide, and acquire new and/or develop existing intervention skills (Public Health Agency, 2011). A recent evaluation of the ASIST programme in the Republic and Northern Ireland demonstrated a number of positive outcomes including that it improved participant's knowledge and skills, improved their attitudes towards suicide intervention and increased their willingness to intervene if someone was suicidal (Public Health Agency, 2011).

School-based gatekeeper training programmes can also be useful to help peers and adults to identify at-risk youth in the school environment and provide them with the knowledge and skills to intervene if required. A peer programme to help young people to recognise self-injury in their peers was discussed earlier in this chapter. There are also programmes aimed at adults in the school environment including teachers, school counsellors, school nurses and support staff. However, while evaluation of these programmes has shown that they improve participants' confidence to recognise warning signs and to intervene if necessary, it is not known whether this confidence translates to actual behaviour (Lake & Gould, 2011).

Mental health problems and suicide prevention

As identified in Chapter 3, there is a significant link between mental health problems and suicide and self-harm. There are therefore opportunities for suicide prevention by responding to both diagnosed and undiagnosed mental health problems in a timely and appropriate manner. Primary care provides a key setting for suicide prevention as many people present to their GPs in the weeks and months leading up to their suicide. Luoma et al. (2002) found that 45% of people had contact with their primary care provider within one month of their suicide. In many cases, the presentation is not mental health related, nonetheless these presentations provide the opportunity for GPs and primary care teams to assess and intervene if required. Consequently, an improvement in depression recognition and treatment and suicide risk assessment by GPs is an important component of suicide prevention (Mann et al., 2005). In response to this, many countries now provide specialist training for primary care staff in detecting and managing suicidal risk. In addition to a focus on depression, programmes targeted at the recognition and management of early (first episode) psychosis are shown to have better outcomes and reduced suicidal behaviour for the person experiencing psychosis (McGirr & Turecki, 2011).

For those who require hospitalisation for treatment of their mental health problem, careful discharge planning and follow-up is required. The time after discharge from a mental health unit is known to be one of heightened suicide risk, with most suicides occurring in the first month after discharge, with the peak occurring one week after discharge (Luxton et al., 2013). A review of available literature has shown that post discharge follow-up and intervention can be effective in reducing suicidal behaviour as it may heighten a sense of connectedness and belonging and are reminders of available treatment and routes to seek help (Luxton et al., 2013). It has also been identified that feeling prepared for discharge and having a sense of control over how and when discharge occurs has a major influence on subsequent discharge experience and may potentially reduce the risk of suicidal behaviour post discharge (Cutcliffe et al., 2012).

In addition to responding to mental health problems, it is also important to respond to the *impact* of mental illness on a person. Experiencing social exclusion, that is lack of participation in key social activities, is not uncommon for people with mental health problems and this is frequently as a result of societal stigma about mental health problems. Consequently, suicide prevention should focus to some degree on important initiatives which aim to increase social support. In this regard family and friends have to be mobilised and social support from available communities needs to be optimised (Fleischmann & Shekhar, 2013). The provision of educational activities to teach effective coping skills and problem solving is also seen as important.

Responding to self-harm

It is widely recognised that one of the strongest predictors of completed suicide is a history of self-harm. The World Health Organisation have identified that those who present with self-harm in clinical practice are not being managed effectively and evidence-based practice is not being implemented (Fleischmann & Shekhar, 2013). Considering the strong link between self-harm and completed suicide, it is imperative that those who engage in self-harm are assessed and, if appropriate, referred for treatment. This can be difficult in light of the fact that most self-harm is hidden and therefore most who engage in it never come to the attention of health professionals. For this reason, outreach initiatives are required to target this predominately adolescent group. However, of those who do present for hospital treatment for self-harm, most come through Emergency Departments (EDs) and present with often serious self-harm behaviours. Therefore, EDs, and the staff within them, are very well positioned to provide assessment and interventions to those who present with self-harm. However, while ED staff may be well-positioned to assess those who present with suicidal behaviour, it appears that many do not feel confident in this role (Doyle et al., 2007). As a response to this, there are a number of initiatives which involve the education and training of staff in the ED to better prepare them to identify, assess and treat those who present having self-harmed. In addition to providing training to general medical staff who work in the ED, there are also initiatives which locate mental health professionals within EDs, or provide a follow-up outreach service for those who present with self-harm and leave following medical treatment. Maintaining regular follow-up contact is essential for the management of self-harm (Fleischmann & Shekhar, 2013). All of these strategies are designed to ensure that those presenting to EDs for treatment of self-harm are assessed and referred for appropriate treatment if required. However, it has been identified that the assessment procedures for those presenting to the ED having self-harmed is inconsistent both within and between countries (Arensman et al., 2011) suggesting room for improvement in this important suicide prevention initiative. Care of the person who is presenting to the ED for treatment of self-harm/suicidal behaviour is discussed further in Chapter 10.

In situations where self-harm is associated with a diagnosis of a personality disorder, there is evidence to suggest that Dialectical Behaviour Therapy (DBT) has promising results. DBT is a form of psychotherapy which focuses on facilitating the learning of distress tolerance skills incorporating a number of key principles including mindfulness (Feigenbaum, 2008). Randomised controlled trials of DBT have shown it to reduce self-harm, suicidal ideation and suicide attempts in addition to reducing visits to the ED for treatment of self-harm (Linehan et al., 2006).

Marginalised groups

There are groups of people in society who are known to have higher levels of suicide and self-harm than the rest of the population. Included here are Lesbian, Gay, Bisexual and Transgender (LGBT) people (King et al., 2008), Gypsy and Traveller groups (Cemlyn et al., 2009), prisoners (Fazel et al., 2011) and long-term unemployed (Milner et al., 2013). Marginalised groups such as these often experience discrimination and in some cases health and social inequalities which may make them more vulnerable to suicidal behaviour and self-harm. Suicide prevention initiatives which focus on developing supports to counteract the vulnerability to suicidal behaviour and self-harm are required and have been developed in many countries, particularly in Western societies. In addition to focusing on these 'at-risk' groups within the context of suicide prevention, there is another group who require particular support and that is those who have been bereaved by suicide – the suicide survivors. This issue is considered in the next chapter.

Reducing repetitive self-harm through harm reduction

Many of the suicide prevention interventions detailed above feed into the prevention of self-harm in addition to the prevention of completed suicide on a broad scale. However, there is a need to consider the issue of 'self-harm prevention' on an individual level for those who already engage in self-harm. The NICE guidelines on the short-term physical and psychological management and secondary prevention of self-harm in primary and secondary care (NICE, 2004) recommend that harm minimisation issues and techniques and alternative coping strategies are discussed with those who repeatedly self-harm. It is the case that for many people attempting to stop self-harm through prevention and control may be counterproductive and actually increase risk for individuals as it restricts someone's primary coping mechanism (Inckle, 2011). An alternative to this approach is offered in the form of harm reduction, sometimes called harm minimisation. Harm reduction is about the person accepting the need to self-harm to survive until survival is possible by other means (Pembroke, 2007), while preventing unwanted, irreversible and possibly fatal harm. Some harm reduction strategies include the following:

- *Education*: Education to minimise unwanted and possible fatal risks is an important component of harm minimisation. This includes the provision of reliable and accessible information on the degree of risk associated with various methods of self-harm. Much of this information is produced by user-led and voluntary services (Inckle, 2011). The Bristol Crisis Service for Women is one such service which produces a range of information to help people who self-harm, including *The Rainbow Journal* which is aimed at helping young women move 'from self-harm to self-care'.
- *Aftercare and wound treatment*: It is known that many people who self-harm do not come to the attention of health care professionals. In this context, it is important that those who self-harm have information on how best to manage their wounds to avoid infection and further complications.
- *Preventing and reducing scars*: The Royal College of Psychiatrists (2007) provide information on harm reduction strategies including education and advice on aftercare as mentioned previously. In addition to this, they provide advice on preventing, reducing and disguising scars which is important to some.

In addition to harm minimisation strategies, Tantam and Huband (2009) identify a number of known distraction strategies or strategies which may provide safer alternatives to self-harm for some people. These include the following:

- Physical activity such as walking, running or mental activity such as card games or puzzles.
- Listening to music, watching a film.
- Marking skin with red ink which can act as a temporary substitute to skin cutting.
- Gripping an ice-cube firmly in the hand. The discomfort this produces can be a temporary substitute for self-harm for some people.
- Wearing an elastic band on the wrist that is snapped when the person has an urge to self-harm. Again, this uncomfortable sensation may substitute for self-harm without causing damage to the skin.

The growth of online support for self-harm

The Internet is a widely used source of support for many health-related issues and has become an increasingly popular source of support, information and advice for those who self-harm. Chapter 5 has identified a number of mainly service-user-led online support services and charities which aim to provide information about self-harm and recovery. The information provided includes tips on coping with stress, helpful links and resources, advice on choosing a relevant therapy, and some provide moderated online support groups. These online supports may be particularly useful for those who struggle with talking face-to-face about their self-harm (Tantam & Huband, 2009). There are also advantages in terms of accessibility, anonymity and confidentiality. In addition to these online information and support services offered by known service user organisations, there has been a growth in 'e-message' boards which are largely unmoderated virtual communities for those who self-harm. A study by Jonhson et al. (2010) of an e-message board on self-harm found that almost half of the participants visited at least once a day and more than half reported that their self-harm had reduced in frequency since joining the virtual community. This may be associated with the increase in social support and sense of community in individuals who feel isolated by their behaviour. However, a note of caution is required here. While the Internet has much potential to provide information and increase social support and a sense of belonging, it is also associated with many potential risks. It has been identified that sharing pictures, videos and detailed descriptions of self-harm can reinforce self-harm behaviour in addition to triggering urges in some people (Lewis et al., 2012). In these instances instead of offering support and hope for recovery, information on the Internet can serve as a trigger for vulnerable individuals to initiate or continue self-harm.

> ## CASE SCENARIO 8.1
>
> Amy is a 20-year-old woman who attends college and works part-time. She started harming herself by cutting her forearm about two years ago when she was finding it difficult to make the transition from school to college. Cutting made her feel better but only for a while after which the anxiety and feelings of stress would re-emerge. After a period of time, life settled down for Amy in college, she gets good grades and has made a few good, close friends. However, she still has the urge to cut herself when she is faced with a particularly difficult situation and has done so on a number of occasions. She regularly sees a counsellor in college to help her manage her feelings of stress and anxiety. Recently, a row with her boyfriend and stress about a number of college assignments due in at the same time have made her feel tense and wound-up and she feels the need to self-harm again. She explains this to her counsellor at her next appointment.

- What factors contribute to Amy's urge to self-harm?
- What could the counsellor advise her to do instead of self-harming when feeling tense?
- How might the counsellor help Amy work through an episode of self-harm while reducing the risk of unwanted and serious self-harm?
- What additional sources of support may be available to Amy to supplement the support she received from her counsellor?

Conclusion

There is now widespread recognition of suicide and self-harm as a global public health problem which causes significant distress at individual, community and broader societal level. This has led to national suicide prevention policies being developed in many countries all over the world. As a result, great strides have been made over the past two decades in the area of suicide and self-harm prevention. Increased research in the area of suicidology has identified a number of evidence-based prevention programmes which appear to show positive outcomes. However, there is still some way to go. While many suicide and self-harm prevention initiatives have been positively evaluated, others have equivocal findings where it is unclear exactly how effective they have been. For that reason, there is a requirement to determine the efficacy of all suicide and self-harm prevention initiatives and the degree to which they are generalisable across different populations. The existing challenge in suicide prevention is to 'improve knowledge of what works and what does not work in suicide prevention' (O'Connor et al., 2011: 630). Although suicide (and self-harm) will never be completely eliminated, incorporating evidence-based suicide and self-harm prevention initiatives into practice can lead to significant reductions thereby minimising the unique distress caused by this tragic and often avoidable outcome.

REFLECTIVE QUESTIONS

1. What general population approaches to preventing and reducing suicide and self-harm have been implemented in your country? Give examples.
2. What targeted approaches to preventing and reducing suicide and self-harm have been implemented in your country? Give examples.
3. What challenges (if any) have been encountered in implementing the above approaches? Give examples.
4. What role do you think you can play in suicide and self-harm prevention on a local level?

REFERENCES

Arensman, E., Corcoran, P. and Fitzgerald, A.P. (2011) Deliberate self-harm: Extent of the problem and prediction of repetition. In O'Connor, R.C., Platt, S. and Gordon, J. (eds.) *International Handbook of Suicide Prevention. Research, Policy and Practice*. West Sussex: Wiley-Blackwell, pp 119–132.

Cemlyn, S., Greenfields, M., Burnett, S., Matthews, Z. and Whitwell, C. (2009) *Inequalities Experience by Gypsy and Traveller Communities: A Review*. Manchester: Equality and Human Rights Commission.

Chapple, A., Ziebland, S., Simkin, S. and Hawton, K. (2013) How people bereaved by suicide perceive newspaper reporting: Qualitative study. *The British Journal of Psychiatry*, 203: 228–232.

Chen, Y.-Y., Bennewith, O., Hawton, K., Simkin, S., Cooper, J., Kapur, N. and Gunnell, D. (2013) Suicide by burning barbeque charcoal in England. *Journal of Public Health,* 35(2): 223–227.

Corcoran, P., Reulbach, U., Keeley, H.S., Perry, I.J., Hawton, K. and Arensman, E. (2010). Use of analgesics in intentional drug overdose presentation to hospital before and after the withdrawal of distalgesic from the Irish market. *BMC Clinical Pharmacology,* 10: 6. doi: 10.1186/1472-6904-10-6.

Cutcliffe, J.R., Links, P.S., Harder, H.G., Balderson, K., Bergmans, Y., Eynan, R., Ambree, M. and Nisenbaum, R. (2012) Understanding the risks of recent discharge. *Crisis,* 33(1): 21–29.

Doyle, L., Keogh, B. and Morrissey, J. (2007) Caring for patients with suicidal behaviour: An exploratory study. *British Journal of Nursing,* 16(19): 1218–1222.

Dumesnil, H. and Verger, P. (2009) Public awareness campaigns about depression and suicide: A review. *Psychiatric Services,* 60(9): 1203–1213.

European Commission and World Health Organisation. (2008) European pact for mental health and well-being. *EU High-Level Conference: Together for Mental Health and Well-being.* Brussels: European Commission.

Fazel, S., Grann, M., Kling, B. and Hawton, K. (2011) Prison suicide in 12 countries: An ecological study of 861 suicides during 2003–2007. *Social Psychiatry and Psychiatric Epidemiology,* 46: 191–195.

Feigenbaum, J. (2008) Dialectical behaviour therapy. *Psychiatry,* 7(3): 112–116.

Fleischmann, A. and Shekhar, S. (2013) Suicide prevention in the WHO mental health gap action programme (mhGAP). *Crisis,* 34(5): 295–296.

Gunnell, D., Nowers, M. and Bennewith, O. (2005a) Suicide by jumping: Is prevention possible? *Suicidologi,* 10(2).

Gunnell, D., Bennewith, O., Hawton, K., Simkin, S. and Kapur, N. (2005b) The epidemiology and prevention of suicide by hanging: A systematic review. *International Journal of Epidemiology,* 34: 433–432.

Hadlaczky, G., Wasserman, D., Hoven, C.W., Mandell, D.J. and Wasserman, C. (2011) Suicide prevention strategies: Case studies from across the globe. In O'Connor, R.C., Platt, S. and Gordon, J. (eds.) *International Handbook of Suicide Prevention. Research, Policy and Practice.* West Sussex: Wiley-Blackwell.

Hawton, K., Bergen, H., Simkin, S., Wells, C., Kapur, N. and Gunnell, D. (2012) Six-year follow-up of impact of co-proxamol withdrawal in England and Wales on prescribing and deaths: Time-series study. *PLoS Med,* 9(5): e1001213. doi: 10.1371/journal.pmed.1001213.

Inckle, K (2011) The first cut is the deepest: A hard-reduction approach to self-injury. *Social Work in Mental Health,* 9(5): 364–378.

Johnson, G.M., Zastawny, S. and Kulpa, A. (2010) E-message boards for those who self-injure: Implications for E-health. *International Journal of Mental Health and Addiction,* 8(4): 566–569.

King, M., Semlyen, J., See Tai, S., Killaspy, H., Osborn, D., Popelyuk, D. and Nazareth, I. (2008) A systematic review of mental disorder, suicide, and deliberate self-harm in lesbian, gay and bisexual people. *BMC Psychiatry,* 8: 70 doi: 10.1186/1471-244X-8-70

Lake, A.M. and Gould, M.S. (2011) School-based strategies for youth suicide prevention. In O'Connor, R.C., Platt, S. and Gordon, J. (eds.) *International Handbook of Suicide Prevention. Research, Policy and Practice.* West Sussex: Wiley-Blackwell.

Lewis, S.P., Heath, N.L., Michal, N.J. and Duggan, J.M. (2012) Non-suicidal self-injury, youth, and the internet: What mental health professionals need to know. *Child and Adolescent Psychiatry and Mental Health*, 6: 13. doi: 10.1186/1753-2000-6-13.

Linehan, M.M., Comtois, K.A., Murray, A.M., Brown, M.Z., Gallop, R.J., Heard, H.L., Korslund, K.E., Tutek, D.A., Reynolds, S.K. and Lindenboim, N. (2006) Two-year randomized controlled trial and follow-up of dialectical behaviour therapy vs therapy by experts for suicidal behaviors and borderline personality disorder. *Archives of General Psychiatry*, 63(7): 757–766.

Luoma, J.B., Martin C.E. and Pearson, J.L. (2002) Contact with mental health and primary care providers before suicide: A review of the evidence. *American Journal of Psychiatry*, 159(6): 909–916.

Luxton, D.D., June, J.D. and Comtois, K.A. (2013) Can postdischarge follow-up contacts prevent suicide and suicidal behavior? *Crisis*, 34(1): 32–41.

Machlin, A., Pirkis, J. and Spittal, M.J. (2013) Which Suicides are reported in the media – and what makes them 'Newsworthy'? *Crisis*, 34(5): 305–313.

Mann, J.J., Apter, A., Bertolote, J., Beautrais, A., PhD; Currier, A., Haas, A, Hegerl, U., Lonnqvist, J., Malone, K., MD; Marusic, A., Mehlum, L., Patton, G., Phillips, M., Rutz, W., Rihmer, Z., Schmidtke, A., Shaffer, D., Silverman, M., Takahashi, Y., Varnik, A., Wasserman, D., Yip, P. and Hendin, H. (2005) Suicide prevention strategies: A systematic review. *Journal of the American Medical Association*, 294(16): 2064–2074.

McGirr, A. and Turecki, G. (2011) Schizophrenia, other psychotic disorders, and suicidal behaviour. In O'Connor, R.C., Platt, S. and Gordon, J. (eds.) *International Handbook of Suicide Prevention. Research, Policy and Practice*. West Sussex: Wiley-Blackwell.

Milner, A., Page, A. & LaMontagne, A.D. (2013) Long term unemployment and suicide: A systematic review and meta-analysis. *PLoS One*, 8(1):e51333. doi: 10.1371/journal.pone.0051333.

Morey, C., Corcoran, P., Arensman, E and Perry, I.J. (2008) The prevalence of self-reported deliberate self-harm in Irish adolescents. *BMC Public Health*, 8(79).

Muehlenkamp, J.J., Walsh, B.W. and McDade, M. (2010) Preventing non-suicidal self-injury in adolescents: The signs of self-injury program. *Journal of Youth and Adolescence*, 39: 306–314.

National Collaborating Centre for Mental Health. (2004) *Clinical Guideline 16. Self-Harm: The Short Term Physical and Psychological Management and Secondary Prevention of Self-harm in Primary and Secondary Care*. London: National Institute for Clinical Excellence.

O'Connor, R.C., Platt, S. and Gordon, J. (2011) Achievements and challenges in suicidology: Conclusions and future directions. In O'Connor, R.C., Platt, S. and Gordon, J. (eds.) *International Handbook of Suicide Prevention. Research, Policy and Practice*. West Sussex: Wiley-Blackwell.

Pearson, J.L. (2011) Challenges in US suicide prevention public awareness programmes. In O'Connor, R.C., Platt, S. and Gordon, J. (eds.) *International Handbook of Suicide Prevention. Research, Policy and Practice*. West Sussex: Wiley-Blackwell.

Pembroke, L. (2007). Harm-minimisation: Limiting the damage of self-injury. In Spandler, R.C. and Warner, S. (eds.) *Beyond Fear and Control: Working with Young People Who Self-harm*. Ross-on-Wye: PCCS books.

Public Health Agency. (2011) *All Island Evaluation of Applied Suicide Intervention Skills Training (ASIST)*. Belfast: Public Health Agency.

Royal College of Psychiatrists. (2007) *Self-harm: Limiting the Damage*. Better Services for People who Self-Harm.

Shaffer, D., Garland, A., Vaeland, V., Underwood, M.M, and Busner, C. (1991) The impact of curriculum-based suicide prevention program for teenagers. *Journal of the American Academy of Child and Adolescent Psychiatry,* 30: 588–596.

Tantam, D. and Huband, N. (2009) *Understanding Repeated Self-injury: A Multidisciplinary Approach.* New York: Palgrave MacMillan.

World Health Organisation. (2010) *Global Strategy to Reduce the Harmful Use of Alcohol.* Geneva: World Health Organisation.

World Health Organisation. (2012) *Public Health Action for the Prevention of Suicide: A Framework.* Geneva: World Health Organisation.

Yip, P.S.F., Law, C.K., Fu, K-W., Law, Y.W., Wong, P.W.C. and Xu, Y. (2010) Restricting the means of suicide by charcoal burning poisoning. *British Journal of Psychiatry,* 196: 241–242.

Yip, P.S.F., Caine, E., Yousuf, S., Chang, S-S., Wu, K. C-C. and Chen, Y-Y. (2012) Means restriction for suicide prevention. *Lancet,* 379: 2393–2399.

CHAPTER 9

Postvention

Brian Keogh

Introduction

The death of a loved one by suicide has a far-reaching and complex impact on those who have come to be known as suicide survivors. According to Andriessen (2009: 43), a suicide survivor is 'a person who has lost a significant other (or a loved one) by suicide, and whose life is changed because of the loss'. The aim of this chapter is to introduce the reader to the concept of postvention. It will focus on strategies that can be used to assist individuals who have been affected by suicide, in particular, family, friends and members of the community. It will begin by defining postvention and outlining the needs of people who have been bereaved by suicide. It will then briefly examine grief theory and introduce the reader to the concept of complicated grief. The chapter will offer some strategies from a professional and lay perspective which may assist suicide survivors in the days and months following the death of a loved one. In addition, responding to a death from suicide within a school or workplace will be considered. While the emphasis in this chapter will be on interventions following a death from suicide, some strategies for postvention in terms of self-harm will also be presented. Self-care strategies to assist those working with people who complete suicide or who engage in self-harm have been discussed in Chapter 7 and can be used in conjunction with some of the strategies presented here.

LEARNING OUTCOMES

By the end of this chapter, you should be better able to:

1. define the term 'postvention' and examine its meaning in the context of support for individuals bereaved by suicide;
2. describe how grief manifests in people who have been bereaved by suicide;
3. outline the needs of people who have been bereaved by suicide;
4. examine strategies that can be useful to assist people who have been bereaved by suicide within formal and informal networks.

Who are suicide survivors and what is postvention?

In this context, a suicide survivor is someone who has been bereaved by suicide. Sometimes this term is given to those individuals who have attempted suicide and survived or to those who have had suicidal thoughts in the past. This is not the intention here. Andriessen and Krysinska (2012) suggest that there is a difference between someone who is a suicide survivor and someone who is exposed to suicide. On one hand, they suggest that the term 'suicide survivor' means that the bereaved and the deceased share a relationship and that the impact of the suicide will depend on the closeness of that relationship. On the other hand, exposure to suicide suggests that the individual is affected by the suicide, but did not know the person who died. Postvention has been described as activities which can be utilised to support and help people who have been bereaved by suicide (Trimble et al., 2012). In the words of Shneidman (1999: 447), 'postvention consists of those activities that serve to reduce the aftereffects of a traumatic event in lives of survivors'. The death of a person by suicide will often have a ripple effect, impacting differently on individual, family and community members. In this sense, postvention activities can also be described as suicide prevention strategies, as their intention is also to reduce suicide as well as providing support. In this chapter, the focus will be on postvention activities designed to support individual and families, although some references will be made to supporting communities.

Grief and complicated grief

Grief refers to the broad range of feelings and behaviours that follow a death (Worden, 2004). Worden (2004) goes on to describe a spectrum of grief manifestations that may emerge in the days, weeks and months following bereavement. These manifestations are outlined in Table 9.1.

Many authors, when discussing grief, discuss it in terms of it being a process that follows a number of interrelated and fluid stages. While no two people will experience grief the same way and there is no consensus about the intensity or duration of 'grieving', Zisook and Shear (2009) suggest that individuals can move from acute grief to integrated or abiding grief. While this suggests that the grief process is unending, it does highlight that the bereaved can learn to live with the loss rather than forgetting about or disregarding the loved one who has died (Zisook & Shear, 2009). This corresponds with Worden's conceptualisation of grief as a set of tasks, the final ones being to adjust to the environment in which the deceased is missing and to emotionally relocate the deceased and move on with life (Worden, 2004: 32–35). Achieving this, according to Jordan (2009), involves a transformation of the relationship with the deceased rather than a letting go or release. There is some debate in the literature regarding the differences and similarities to bereavement following suicide and bereavement following other types of sudden deaths. However, Console (2012) suggest that those left behind following a suicide experience a

Table 9.1   Manifestations of grief (Worden, 2004: 11–20)

Sadness	Anger	Guilt and self reproach	Anxiety	Loneliness
Fatigue	Helplessness	Shock	Yearning	Emancipation
Relief	Hollowness in the stomach	Tightness in the chest/throat	Oversensitivity to noise	Depersonalisation
Breathlessness	Weakness	Lack of energy	Dry mouth	Disbelief
Confusion	Preoccupation	Sense of presence	Hallucinations	Sleep disturbances
Appetite disturbances	Absentmindedness	Social withdrawal	Dreams of the deceased	Avoidance
Searching	Sighing	Restless over activity	Crying	Seeking reminders of the deceased

different type of grief which is often permeated with intense feelings of guilt, anger and confusion. Furthermore, they argue that those bereaved by suicide may be at an increased risk of suicide, heightening the need for responses that are sensitive, specific and accessible. In the immediate hours and days after the suicide, feelings such as intense shock, disbelief, numbness and a sense of unreality are normal reactions to sudden death (Dyregrov et al., 2012). Longer term reactions should also be perceived as normal and interpreted as the individual's way of coming to terms with the bereavement and learning to cope with and process the death (Dyregrov & Dyregrov, 2008). Grad (2011) suggests that while there are many grief processes that are universal, the grief following a suicide has a unique course that is different for each person experiencing it. While some of these processes mirror experiences following any death, they are unique in the ways that they emerge and the reasons that they manifest. Jordan (2001) suggests that grief reactions following a suicide differ in three broad themes.

1. Survivors experience greater difficulty when trying to make sense of the death.
2. Survivors experience a greater level of guilt and may feel in some way responsible for the death. For example, they may feel that they should have been able to stop the person from dying.
3. Survivors may experience a level of abandonment, anger or rejection that may not manifest in other sudden death situations.

The following fictitious case scenario illustrates the grief reactions experienced by a person following a suicide.

> **CASE SCENARIO 9.1**
>
> Tina felt so angry towards her father who had died by suicide six months ago. As an only child, she was very close to her dad and they had become particularly close since the death of her mother over ten years ago. She visited him weekly and they talked about everything. He enjoyed seeing his grandchildren and talking about them to his friends and neighbours. At times, Tina wondered whether she really knew her father; she feared that other family members might blame her for not noticing that he was unhappy. She thought about their last visit and retraced everything that he said, trying to find something that might explain his suicide. She frequently stated, 'why didn't you say something or leave me a note?'

Complicated grief

Complicated grief, according to Zisook and Shear (2009), occurs when the bereaved individual does not move from acute to integrated grief and affects about 10% of bereaved people. Individuals who are bereaved by suicide may be more prone to complicated grief as the death may be perceived as an abandonment or rejection often evoking strong emotions including anger and unworthiness (Jordan, 2009). While there is a lack of consensus about what constitutes complicated grief, there is general agreement that it exists, and that for some people, moving through the grieving process is more difficult. Furthermore, the symptoms of complicated grief are similar to 'uncomplicated grief', making accurate diagnosis and treatment difficult. In addition, the manifestations of grief are so variable in intensity and duration, individuals may feel that they are grieving in a complicated way but their feelings may be within the normal range of emotional responses that are an appropriate reaction to the events that have occurred. In some cases, professional help may be required and individuals may benefit from speaking to a therapist about what has happened. Other people may feel anxious and depressed; while non-pharmacological approaches such as counselling and support are preferable, they may benefit from medications and should consult their general practitioner.

The needs of people who have been bereaved by suicide

Grad (2012) suggests that the aim of postvention interventions is to assist individuals with understanding, accepting and emotionalising the loss of the person from suicide. Interventions comprise of individual, family or group help which can be delivered in a professional or lay capacity (Grad, 2011). Trimble et al.'s (2012) small study about postvention experiences in Ireland found that the participants who were bereaved by suicide valued community-based supports in the period following the loss. This involved informal exchanges such as people calling in and offering support or practical assistance with issues such as finance. This is supported by Dyregrov et al. (2012) who describe this sort of support as 'social network support' and they believe it is invaluable in protecting the mental health of individuals during this difficult time.

Consequently, harnessing the informal supports that exist within the affected individual's extended family, friends and community are essential to achieve effective coping. In the United Kingdom, The Department of Health (2006) in their document 'Help is at hand' and Doughty (2007) provide some advice for friends and colleagues on how to respond when someone they know is bereaved by suicide:

- Make contact with the person and let them know that you are there for them.
- Ask them what they would like you to do for them.
- Provide them with the opportunity to talk but be careful not to press them for too much information or to talk about the events if they feel they are not ready.
- When talking about the deceased, use their name and share stories and memories about them.
- Don't think that the person will grieve in a certain way or tell them to think positively.
- Try not to make assumptions about the person or the manner in which they died.
- Be careful about talking about the person 'committing' suicide.
- Offer practical help such as running errands or doing some shopping.
- Remember that the bereaved person will probably receive lots of support in the days and weeks following the death; however, this might taper off and the person may find that they need more support in the months and years after the event. There may be times that are particularly difficult such as birthdays, Christmas and anniversaries when your support will be appreciated.
- Involve the person in social activities. Even if they, refuse continue to ask them.

According to the American Association of Suicidology (2004), the most helpful and important thing for suicide survivors is having someone to listen to them. While it is acknowledged that this can be difficult, relatives and friends are encouraged to allow survivors to tell their stories and to listen in a non-judgemental way. According to Lukas and Seiden (1987), listening is important as it allows the survivor to talk and to focus on what the events mean to them. Non-judgemental listening involves demonstrating that you understand and are there for the person. In addition, avoiding the use of clichés or giving unwanted advice will convey that you are interested in the person and want to support them at this time.

The Health Service Executive (2006: 7) in Ireland has also produced a document called 'You are not alone'. In it they list some strategies that families have found useful when bereaved by suicide:

- Learning to mourn
- Acknowledging all feelings
- Talking honestly with family and friends

- Having a regular chat and check-up with a doctor
- Reviewing pictures and mementos
- Visiting the grave
- Rearranging and storing the belongings of the deceased
- Writing a letter to the deceased
- Being able to be angry but accepting that you love the person who died
- Meeting others with similar experiences.

Peer support

Peer support, according to Dyregrov et al. (2012), is support from other people who have experienced a similar loss. According to Dyregrov and Dyregrov (2008), peer support either through bereavement support groups or through more informal channels allows suicide survivors the space and time to grieve openly in an environment where their experiences and feelings are understood. In addition, survivors may find that being able to provide support to other individuals who have been bereaved by suicide is of mutual benefit. There may also be survivors who may not feel that they are ready or do not wish to engage in peer support. For those individuals, there are a wealth of books, journals and websites that offer readings and reflections that they may be able to draw comfort and support from. In many countries there are also telephone helplines that survivors can access if they wish to do so or if they are unable to access face-to-face services. While information and support will be sufficient for most suicide survivors, it is imperative that those who need to move to the next level of intervention are able to recognise that they need to do so. Individuals involved in peer support can be of assistance in helping survivors recognise the need to seek additional help. This might be necessary if the survivor experiences some of the following:

- Expresses any sort of suicidal ideas or intent.
- Experiences nightmares or cannot sleep.
- Experiences exhaustion, panic, anxiety or other intense feelings.
- Feel overwhelmed by feelings of sadness, guilt or anger.
- Are drinking too much or are relying on drugs for relief.
- Find they have no social network to share their grief with.
- They become self-isolating.
- The intensity of their grief experiences do not diminish over the initial months.

Source: Taken from 'Grieving the suicide of someone close' available from www.console.ie and Dyregrov et al 2012.

The role of professional organisations

According to Jordan (2008), the most commonly used professional interventions are either individual therapy or bereavement support groups. In order to

Table 9.2 Bereavement support service levels (Console, 2012: 10)

Service level	Example of services
One – Information	Suitable for people who experience a normal or mild level of distress. Examples of these services include the distribution of leaflets, books or information websites etc.
Two – Support	Suitable for people who experience a moderate level of distress. Examples include support groups and self-help groups,
Three – Counselling	Suitable for people who experience a severe reaction to the bereavement and is aimed at those who need group or individual counselling over a short period of time.
Four – Psychotherapy	Suitable for those who have a complicated reaction to the bereavement and is aimed at those who have cumulative, complex, longer term problems that need to be addressed on a one to one basis.

assist people who have been bereaved by suicide, it is important to understand what their specific needs are. Console (2012), the National Organisation for supporting people in suicidal crisis and those bereaved by suicide in Ireland, suggests that there are a range of bereavement support services and they have divided them into four categories. While there can be some overlap between the services that are provided in each level, each one plays a role in suicide bereavement support depending on the specific needs of the individuals who use them (Table 9.2).

Console has also developed ten guiding principles that they believe should underpin services that are provided for people who have been bereaved by suicide (Console, 2012: 7):

1. Ensure they 'do no harm' to those who come to them for support.
2. Ensure the needs of the person(s) bereaved by suicide are central to the service/organisation.
3. Ensure the self-care needs and welfare of staff, service providers or support personnel involved with the service/organisation are an important aspect of service governance.
4. Deliver services in an appropriate, safe and helpful manner and environment.
5. Provide services that are readily accessible to those bereaved by suicide.
6. Commit to providing sustainable, consistent and continuous services for the person(s) bereaved by suicide.
7. Promote inclusivity and equality in all dealings with the person(s) bereaved by suicide.
8. Acknowledge that there is a collective responsibility in supporting those bereaved by suicide and draw on and collaborate with communities and other agencies where possible to affect change.
9. Recognise the preventative value of sound suicide postvention practices.

10. Commit to the continuous training, improvement of their services and adhere to best practice standards.

Grad et al. (2004) found that one of the most important things that suicide survivors wanted when dealing with professionals was a more sensitive and compassionate experience. This included professionals having a greater awareness of suicide survivors' needs and an ability to respond to them with tact and sensitivity. While many people working with suicide survivors will have specific education and training or experience in working with survivors, it is likely that the majority of people will meet professionals in the medical, paramedical, police or legal fields. Individuals working in these areas also need to think about how they are perceived by suicide survivors and to ensure that they are non-judgemental and sensitive when interacting with survivors. According to Suicide Prevention Australia (2009), survivors may find that they may get appropriate support within the mental health services; however, they may be reluctant to avail of it if they perceive that the care that their relative has received was in some way inadequate. In terms of communicating with suicide survivors, people working in a professional capacity may find some of the strategies listed earlier useful.

Responding to a suicide within a school or workplace

In the event of a suicide within a school or workplace it is imperative that a postvention protocol is in place and that staff and students are aware of the support networks that are available within the school or organisation. As with all postvention measures, tact, sensitivity and honesty are crucial to ensuring that individuals feel supported. In schools, teachers need to be able to target vulnerable students who may be at risk of attempting suicide while maintaining a sense of routine in the hours and days following the death. A planned and consistent approach from all personnel will prevent excessive dramatisation of the suicide or the perpetuation of myths about the deceased or the manner in which they died. In the weeks following the suicide, plans for a memorial service may help the school to heal and grow following the death (Samaritans, 2013). Further information about responding to suicide in the school setting is detailed in Chapter 10.

Similarly in the workplace, having a clear protocol in terms of postvention strategies is crucial in the event of a death by suicide of an employee. As with interventions in schools, the death should be treated with sensitivity and honesty while being cognisant of the dignity and privacy of the deceased and their family (Carson J Spencer Foundation, 2013). Managers need to listen to the needs of their employees while making sure supports are made available to those that require them. Decisions should be made about who will attend the funeral and if flowers and cards are to be given to the family. Employees should be allowed to decide these things themselves and time should be made available for staff to attend church or funeral services as appropriate (Austin & McGuinness, 2012). In time a memorial service may facilitate healing and this might be considered by the organisation (Suicide Prevention Resource Centre, 2004). Any discussion regarding a memorial service should be approached with inclusiveness and be kept as simple as possible (Austin & McGuinness, 2012).

The role of the media

Niederkrotenthaler et al. (2010) suggest that there is evidence that the media reporting of suicide can influence individuals' engagement in suicidal behaviour. This is often referred to as 'copycat' behaviour, 'the Werther effect' or 'contagion' (Niederkrotenthaler et al., 2010; Pirkis et al., 2006; Sudak & Sudak, 2005). In addition, insensitive reporting of suicide can negatively impact on suicide survivors consequently worsening the grief that they experience. For this reason many countries have adopted media guidelines for the sensitive reporting of suicide. Central to these guidelines is the avoidance of language and images that glamorise suicide or that might lead to 'copycat' behaviour. Furthermore, Sisask and Varnik (2012) suggest that misrepresentations of suicide and self-harm in the cinema can mislead the public about the nature of suicide and interfere with suicide prevention programmes. Samaritans have produced guidelines for the media reporting of suicide with the aim of reducing 'copycat' or imitative suicides and to ensure that media coverage is sensitive and appropriate. Their guidance provides the following advice to those working in the media (Samaritans, 2013: 6–9):

- Think about the impact of the coverage on your audience.
- Exercise caution when referring to the methods and context of a suicide.
- Avoid over simplification.
- Steer away from melodramatic depictions of suicide or its aftermath.
- Aim for non-sensationalising, sensitive coverage.
- Consider carefully the placement and illustration of reports.
- Educate and inform.

Further information on these points can be obtained by downloading the full booklet from www.samaritans.org

In Ireland, media guidelines have been produced by Samaritans in conjunction with the Irish Association of Suicidology and these are available for download from www.nosp.ie

Postvention following an incident of self-harm

Working with and communicating with people who engage in self-harm has been covered in chapters 5 and 6 and these strategies may be ongoing beyond the initial episode. Families, friends and professional carers may find the repetitive and persistent nature of self-harm frustrating and may be at a loss as to how to help or show support. Strategies presented in Chapter 7 may also be useful in managing some of these strong emotions should they occur. The following are some points that could be considered in the immediate aftermath of an episode of self-harm and are drawn from the work of Senker (2013, McGough (2012) and the National Self Harm Network (http://www.nshn.co .uk):

- Assess the need for medical intervention and administer first aid as appropriate. In cases of self-poisoning such as in drug overdoses, summon medical help immediately. If you are in any doubt about the severity of the harm inflicted or your ability to assist the person, do not hesitate to summon medical assistance.
- Try not to panic or appear shocked.
- Try to avoid becoming angry at the person who has self-harmed as this may prove counterproductive and be perceived as mutually stressful.
- Offer reassurance and support and tell the person that you are there for them.
- The person who has self-harmed may appreciate you being with them at this time without the need to talk or communicate about the self-harm.
- Try to remain non-judgmental.
- Do not look for answers in the immediate aftermath of a self-harming episode and tell the person that they can talk to you about the self-harm when they are ready to do so.
- Try to learn as much as you can about self-harm so that you can learn to support the individuals as well as understanding some of the reasons that people engage in it.
- Look after your own mental health.

Conclusion

The death of someone from suicide has been described as having a ripple effect, impacting differently on family, friends, classmates, neighbours and the wider community. The range of emotions that emerge in the wake of a suicide for those described as survivors often leave people feeling vulnerable, confused and guilty. Consequently the grieving process can be complicated by the sense of abandonment that survivors often experience and the many unanswered questions that they cannot pose to the deceased. Those close to the deceased will begin a difficult and often unpredictable course to reconciling with their loved ones and will often require support and assistance. What is important to remember is that those bereaved by suicide respond to this support and it is imperative that the bereaved are given an opportunity to talk about their loved ones with a safe and non-judgemental environment.

REFLECTIVE QUESTIONS

1. Thinking about grief and complicated grief, do you think there is any difference between the two? If so what do you think they are?
2. How might you respond to someone who states to you 'that they will never get over' the death of their spouse following their death by suicide?

3. When supporting a person who is bereaved by suicide, how might you convey an emphatic and non-judgemental approach?
4. In your area of work, what policy/guidelines on bereavement support services are available?

REFERENCES

American Association of Suicidology. (2004) *Helping Survivors of Suicide: What Can You Do? Available.* Available at: http://www.suicidology.org/c/document_library/get_file?folderId= 257&name=DLFE-456.pdf accessed 30 August 2013.

Andriessen, K. (2009) Can postvention be prevention? *Crisis,* 30: 43–47.

Andriessen, K. and Krysinska, K. (2012) Essential questions on suicide bereavement and postvention. *International Journal of Environmental Research and Public Health,* 9: 24–32.

Austin, C. and McGuinness, B. (2012) *Breaking the Silence in the Workplace: A Guide for Employers on Responding to Suicide in the Workplace.* Dublin: Console & The Irish Hospice Foundation.

Carson J Spencer Foundation, Crisis Care Network, National Action Alliance for Suicide Prevention and American Association of Suicidology. (2013). *A Manager's Guide to Suicide Postvention in the Workplace: 10 Action Steps for Dealing with the Aftermath of Suicide.* Denver, CO: Carson J Spencer Foundation.

Console, National Office for Suicide Prevention and Turas le Cheile. (2012) *National Quality Standards for the Provision of Suicide Bereavement Services: A Practical Resource.* Dublin: Console, National Office for Suicide Prevention & Turas le Cheile.

Department of Health. (2006) *Help Is at Hand: A Resource for People Bereaved by Suicide and Other Sudden, Traumatic Death.* DOH: National Health Service.

Doughty, C. (2007) *If There's Anything I Can Do .... How to Help Someone Who Has Been Bereaved.* Devon: White Ladder Press Ltd.

Dyregrov, K. and Dyregrov, A. (2008) *Effective Grief and Bereavement Support: The Role of Family, Friends, Colleagues, Schools and Support Professionals.* London: Jessica Kingsley Publishers.

Dyregrov, K., Plyhn, E. and Dieserud, G. (2012) *After the Suicide: Helping the Bereaved to Find a Path from Grief to Recovery.* London: Jessica Kingsley Publishers.

Grad, O. (2011) The sequelae of suicide: survivors. In O'Connor, R., Platt, S. and Gordon, J. (eds.) *International Handbook of Suicide Prevention: Research, Policy and Practice.* Oxford: John Wiley & Sons, Ltd, pp 591–576.

Grad, O., Clark, S., Dyregrov, K. and Andriessen, K. (2004) What helps and what hinders the process of surviving the suicide of somebody close? *Crisis,* 25: 134–139.

Health Service Executive. (2006) *You Are Not Alone: A Guide for Survivors in Managing the Aftermath of a Suicide.* Dublin: HSE.

Jordan, J. (2001) Is suicide bereavement different? A reassessment of the literature. *Suicide and Life-Threatening Behavior,* 31(1): 91–102.

Jordan, J. (2008) Bereavement after suicide. *Psychiatric Annals,* 38(10): 1–6.

Jordan, J. (2009) After suicide: Clinical work with survivors. *Grief Matters, The Australian Journal of Grief and Bereavement,* 12(1): 4–9.

Lukas, C. and Seiden, H. (1987) *Silent Grief: Living in the Wake of Suicide.* London: Papermac.

McGough, G. (2012) *Self Harm: The Essential Guide.* Peterborough: Need 2 Know.

Niederkrotenthaler, T., Voracek, M., Herberth, A., Till, B., Strauss, M., Etzersdorfer, E., Eisenwort, B. and Sonneck, G. (2010) Role of media reports in completed and prevented suicide: Werther v. Papageno effects. *The British Journal of Psychiatry*, 197: 234–243.

Pirkis, J., Blood, W., Beautrais, A., Burgess, P. and Skehan, J. (2006) Media guidelines on the reporting of suicide. *Crisis*, 27(2): 82–87.

Samaritans. (2013) *Help When We Needed It Most: How to Prepare and Respond to Suicide in Schools*. Surrey: Samaritans.

Samaritans. (2013) *Media Guidelines for Reporting Suicide*. Surrey: Samaritans.

Senker, C. (2013) *Self Harm*. London: Raintree.

Shneidman, E. (1999) Postvention: The care of the bereaved. In Leenaars, A. (ed.) *Lives and Deaths: Selections from the Works of Edwin S. Shneidman*. Philadelphia: Taylor & Francis Group, pp 444–456.

Sisask, M. and Varnik, A. (2012) Media roles in suicide prevention: A systematic review. *International Journal of Environmental Research and Public Health*, 9: 123–138.

Sudak, H. and Sudak, D. (2005) The media and suicide. *Academic Psychiatry*, 29(5): 495–499.

Suicide Prevention Australia. (2009) *Position Statement: Suicide Bereavement and Postvention*. New South Wales: SPA.

Suicide Prevention Resource Center. (2004) *After a Suicide: Recommendations for Religious Services and Other Public Memorial Observances*. Newton, MA: Education Development Center, Inc.

Trimble, T., Hannigan, B. and Gaffney, M. (2012) Suicide postvention: Coping, support and transformation. *The Irish Journal of Psychology*, 33(2): 115–121.

Worden, J. (2004) *Grief Counselling and Grief Therapy: A Handbook for the Mental Health Practitioner*. 3rd ed. London: Routledge.

Zisook, S. and Shear, K. (2009) Grief and bereavement: What psychiatrists need to know. *World Psychiatry*, 8: 67–74.

CHAPTER 10

Self-harm and Suicide in Prisons, Schools and Emergency Departments

Louise Doyle

Introduction

Self-harm and suicidal behaviour occurs in a variety of settings and work-places and as a result many workers with no mental health background or training find themselves working with vulnerable or 'at risk' people. The aim of this chapter is to provide these workers with some knowledge about self-harm and suicidal behaviour in these specific locations to help inform their practice. This chapter will focus on three specific workplaces where self-harm and suicidal behaviour are not uncommon: Prisons, Schools and Emergency Departments. This chapter discusses the issue of self-harm and suicide within these areas and will identify location-specific issues that may impact upon self-harm and suicidal behaviour. Drawing upon information provided in this chapter, in addition to chapters 5 and 6, the reader is invited to reflect on case scenarios set in a prison, a school and an Emergency Department. Reflective questions based on each case scenario are located throughout the chapter.

LEARNING OUTCOMES

By the end of this chapter, you should be better able to:

1. identify issues that are relevant to self-harm and suicide in the prison setting;
2. identify issues that are relevant to self-harm and suicide in schools;
3. identify issues that are relevant to self-harm and suicide in Emergency Departments;
4. outline how you might respond to self-harm/suicidal behaviour in whichever setting is relevant to your practice.

Self-harm and suicide in prisons

Self-harm and suicide is not uncommon in the prison population. Studies suggest that between 5% and 6% of male prisoners and 20% and 24% of female prisoners self-harm every year (Hawton et al., 2014), while is it identified that the suicide rates of both male and female prisoners are significantly higher than that of the general population in many countries (Fazel et al., 2011). The provision of adequate and effective suicide prevention initiatives is of utmost importance to reduce the rates of self-harm and suicide in custodial settings. In recognition of this, prisoners are identified as a high-risk group for suicide and self-harm in a number of international suicide prevention policies including those in both the United Kingdom and Ireland and are identified as requiring specific targeted interventions to reduce suicidal behaviour. The reduction of suicide and self-harm rates are repeatedly stated concerns of prison authorities and are increasingly seen to be within the remit of prison staff (Marzano et al., 2013).

There are a number of reasons why self-harm and suicide is higher in prisoners than in the general population including the following:

- *High-risk group:* Before they ever enter custody in prisons, prisoners are a vulnerable population at high risk of suicide. Prisons contain a high number of young males who are socially disenfranchised with poor levels of education and high levels of unemployment. In addition to this there are a high number of prisoners who have pre-existing mental health and substance abuse problems which may have been an influencing factor in their incarceration. As entering prison means a cessation of illicit drug use, the experience of withdrawal can also increase self-harm and suicidal behaviour.
- *Separated from family/friends and support network:* The protective effect of having close friends and family members to confide in and support the person is largely lost in the prison setting, where access to family and friends is significantly decreased.
- *Psychological impact of arrest, committal and sentence:* The stress associated with incarceration and the prospect of a long prison sentence can have a significant psychological impact on a person. This psychological impact is increased when the person is serving a life sentence.
- *Poor mental health services in prisons:* Despite the identification of prisoners as a high-risk group for self-harm and suicidal behaviour, many prisons do not have adequate mental health services to meet the large demand. Differences exist in prisons between the levels of screening for mental health difficulties and more importantly the management of such difficulties.

In addition to the factors that increase self-harm and suicidal risk among prisoners generally, there are also factors about prison life itself that can increase risk when in the prison system and these include the following:

- *Increased times of risk:* There are certain stages during custody where the prisoner is at increased risk of engaging in self-harm and suicidal behaviour and these include the time shortly after initial incarceration, periods follow-ing significant court appearances or changes in status and the period shortly after release. In particular, it has been identified that almost half of all self-inflicted deaths in prison occur within the first month of incarceration (Patton & Borrill, 2005).

- *Low level of purposeful activity:* Having little purposeful activity to engage in is associated with a higher level of self-harm and suicidal behaviour.
- *Occupation of a single cell:* Most episodes of suicide or self-harm in prison occur when the prisoner is in a single cell or when he/she is alone in a double cell.
- *Refusal of parole:* Prisoners who are unsuccessful in gaining parole or pro-gressing towards release are in a higher risk group for self-harm and suicidal behaviour.

While there are specific risk factors associated with imprisonment, there are also a number of protective factors. Liebling (1992) has identified the following as factors protective of suicidal behaviour within the prison setting:

- family support and visits;
- constructive activity within the prison system;
- support from other prisoners;
- support from prison staff and probation officers;
- support from prison visitors from other services;
- having hopes and plans for the future;
- being in a system which has excellent inter-departmental communication;
- staff who are professionally trained and valued by the system.

Preventing and responding to self-harm and suicide in prison

As it is an environment where people are closely monitored, there is potential for real progress on suicide prevention within the prison setting. Chapters 5 and 6 of this book provide information about communicating and responding to people engaging in self-harm and suicidal behaviour and most of these skills are transferable to the prison setting. However, due to the uniqueness of the prison setting, there are a number of other important points to note in terms of preventing and responding to self-harm and suicidal behaviour amongst prisoners including:

- *Screening:* As it has been identified that the early stages post incarceration are the high-risk times for suicidal behaviour, there are actions that can be carried out by prison staff which may decrease this risk. Individuals at risk should be identified at reception with appropriate preventative mea-sures initiated. Screening conducted by a mental health professional is the most common method of identifying those at risk of suicide or self-harm at reception.
- *Close/special monitoring:* Once risk of self-harm and suicidal behaviour has been identified, appropriate care pathways should be put in place (Humber

et al., 2011). This can include special supervision/monitoring in addition to mental health interventions. The nature of monitoring is important to consider. It has been reported that those at risk for self-harm and suicidal behaviour dislike being monitored in the absence of emotional interaction and support.

- *Continued mandatory reporting of self-harm and suicide:* Since 2002, a mandatory reporting system of self-harm in prison was introduced in England and Wales (Hawton et al., 2014). Continued mandatory reporting of self-harm in addition to already mandatory reporting of attempted/completed suicide allows for an accurate identification of the extent of self-harm and suicidal behaviour in prisons and provides baseline information from which to plan appropriate interventions.

- *A good relationship:* The promotion of a good relationship between staff and prisoners has an important role in both preventing and responding appropriately to self-harm and suicidal behaviour. Demonstrating respectful and caring attitudes towards prisoners is crucial to this.

- *Providing activities:* It has been identified that prisoners who have little to do during the day are at higher risk of suicide. Therefore, there is an onus on prisons to ensure that prisoners are busily occupied in activities that are meaningful and provide the prisoner not only with something to do but also an opportunity to improve themselves.

- *Improving attitudes:* One major challenge to improving prisoners' mental health and reducing suicide and self-harm is the negative attitude of prison officers and health care staff working within prisons (Hawton et al., 2013). Stigmatising, hostile or distancing attitudes and behaviours by staff can prevent self-harming individuals from seeking help and can heighten distress and risk levels (Marzano et al., 2013).

- *Increased staff training:* It is clear that the prison environment is a stressful working environment and this is made more stressful by the requirement on prison staff to work with self-harm and suicidal behaviour on a daily basis particularly when there is a perceived lack of training and education on this issue. Participants in a study of staff experiences of repeated self-harm in prisoners identified that dealing with self-harm was challenging and frustrating that they did not have the practical resources and/or skills to deal with it, and that levels of prisoner care may suffer as a result of staff becoming cynical and angry (Marzano et al., 2013). There is therefore an obvious need to support staff who work with prisoners who self-harm in order to ensure the best outcomes for prisoners and staff alike.

- *Reducing access to means:* As identified in Chapter 8, reducing access to means is a common suicide prevention approach. However, a prison setting has more potential than most to effectively do this. Prisoners deemed to be at high risk of suicide may require a 'safer cell' (Patton & Borrill, 2005) which provides less opportunity for self-harm as they contain fixed furniture and are free of ligature points.

- *Preparation for release:* The year following release from prison is known to be a high-risk time for suicide. Resettlement programmes are generally available which educate prisoners about how to return to life outside the prison environment.

CASE SCENARIO 10.1

Matthew is 48 years old. He has recently been remanded to prison for the first time following a serious incident in which he stabbed his wife during an argument while he was heavily under the influence of alcohol. Matthew has a history of alcohol abuse; however, he has no history of violent behaviour and he is very distressed by his assault on his wife whom he says he loves dearly. His wife has indicated that she wishes to leave the marriage. On his second night in prison, Matthew made a serious attempt on his life by suspending himself from a door frame with a ligature while his cellmate was not in the cell. He was found by prison officers and was successfully resuscitated.

- What factors might be identified as important in an initial risk assessment upon arrival to prison?
- Drawing on knowledge gained throughout this book, identify how you might respond to Matthew following his suicide attempt.
- What factors will need to be considered to reduce the risk of Matthew engaging in further suicidal behaviour?

Self-harm and suicide in schools

In most countries, incidence of self-harm peaks during adolescence and there are a number of specific factors that influence self-harm and suicidal behaviour in adolescents which are identified in Chapter 4. A multi-centre school-based study of self-harm in seven countries, including the United Kingdom and Ireland, identified that 13.5% of females and 4.3% of males reported a life-time history of self-harm (Madge et al., 2008). This is a significant number of young people within the school setting who report having engaged in self-harm and is thought to equate to approximately one in ten adolescents or 'three in an average classroom' (Best, 2005).

Consequently, it is clear that those working in schools are not unfamiliar with the concept of adolescent self-harm. Many of these young people will come to the attention of school staff either directly as they may come forward looking for help or indirectly as a friend may seek advice from a teacher on their behalf. How school personnel respond to these students can be critical in terms of both ensuring their continued safety and in guiding them towards appropriate intervention. While self-harm in adolescence is often transient, a significant number of adolescents who self-harm do so repeatedly and have poorer outcomes in terms of mental health and a higher risk of completed suicide (Zahl & Hawton, 2004). Consequently, the detection, assessment and treatment of self-harm in adolescents is important and teachers and other school staff have a role to play in this process.

Detecting and responding to self-harm in schools

Teachers are one group of adults with whom young people spend a considerable amount of time and they are therefore often in a position to detect self-harm and to notice changes in the young person's behaviour. While much self-harm in adolescence is hidden, signs of current or recent self-harming behaviour including scars from cutting may become evident during class and particularly during physical education. If this occurs, teachers need to be cognisant of their response to signs of self-harm. Self-harm may elicit a range of feelings and emotions in school staff including shock, anger, sadness, disbelief, helplessness, guilt, disgust and rejection (Hawton et al., 2006). Best (2005) identifies how teachers in his study of self-harm in the school setting felt an intense anxiety and a feeling that the problem was beyond their competence to deal with. This is an important point and our expectations of teachers in this scenario should be considered. It is not expected that school staff 'treat' or assume a formal counselling role when engaging with a young person who has self-harmed. Once self-harm is detected, however, they do have a role in sign posting further help and intervention available to the student. However, their initial reaction to a discovery or disclosure of self-harm is crucial. An open, non-judgemental attitude and willingness to listen is of paramount importance when responding to a young person who has self-harmed.

Following detection or disclosure of self-harm within the school setting, there ought to be a protocol in place to effectively manage the situation. The following are guidelines detailing the ways school staff can respond to a young person who has self-harmed. These guidelines have been broadly informed by those developed by the Oxfordshire Adolescent Self-Harm Forum (2002) (Hawton et al., 2006).

- If you find a student who has self-harmed, be calm and provide reassurance. Follow the first aid guidelines of your school. If the self-harm involves an overdose, medical assessment is required at the Emergency Department.
- Ensure the young person understands the limits of confidentiality if they disclose self-harm. Discuss with them the importance of letting his/her parents know and their fears regarding this.
- Inform the parents of the student's disclosure or the incident of self-harm. This is discussed further below in the context of confidentiality.
- Be aware of your reaction: ensure you have a non-judgemental and open attitude to the young person.
- Assess for risk of further imminent and serious self-harm and refer to Emergency Department.
- Offer information about support agencies that specialise in mental health and are youth orientated.
- Help the young person to identify their own support network (e.g. family, responsible friends) who can help them through difficult times.
- Support peers and be aware of the increased risk of self-harm within the peer group.
- Record any incident of actual self-harm or disclosure of self-harm.

Preventing self-harm/suicidal behaviour in the school setting

As schools are locations where most young people spend considerable periods of time, they can play an important role in decreasing and preventing self-harm and suicidal behaviour in young people and in the promotion of positive mental health. The following are some initiatives schools can undertake in this regard:

- *Develop a self-harm policy:* All schools should have a policy for responding to self-harm which provides teachers with a clear roadmap for working with the distressed student. This policy should include guidance on how to liaise with local health services in both emergency and routine situations and also about the limits of confidentiality between school personnel and students. The issue of the level of confidentiality to be maintained with a young person in a school setting can be a contentious but important one for students, teachers/counsellors and parents alike. In the case of school counsellors, absolute confidentiality cannot be guaranteed to students within a counselling session, as exceptions (e.g. potential of harm to student) are mandated in ethical codes. Similar exceptions to confidentiality exist between teachers and students, and for this reason teachers need to be clear about the limits of confidentiality and this is particularly pertinent when dealing with self-harm and suicidal behaviour. It should be made very clear to students under what circumstances confidentiality cannot be kept and that parents may be informed of staff concerns.
- *Supervision and de-brief of staff:* Working with students who self-harm or experiencing a suicide of a student can be very traumatic for school personnel and the emotional impact can at times be overwhelming. In order for them to continue to work in such circumstances, it is important that they are given the opportunity to de-brief from their experience with the support from colleagues and management. Chapter 7 of this book provides some guidelines in relation to self-care when working in this area.
- *Education for teachers:* Education and training provision in the area of self-harm for teachers and other school staff is at best patchy (Best, 2005). There is therefore a requirement for special training courses which focus on understanding self-harm and suicidal behaviour and identifying and supporting students who may be vulnerable or at risk.
- *Education for students:* School provides an opportunistic setting to reach out to large numbers of young people and is a prime location for the delivery of mental health promotion initiatives. Much has been written about the potential for schools to deliver education programmes for students about suicide, self-harm and mental health in general. While there are concerns about some school-based programmes which focus exclusively on suicide (Shaffer et al., 1991), there is consensus that more general evidence-based mental health education programmes which aim to improve resilience and coping can have beneficial effects for young people (Lake & Gould, 2011).
- *Helping peers:* It is known that young people are more likely to disclose self-harm to a friend than to any other person. It is also known however that

young people often feel ill-equipped to deal with disclosure of a friend's self-harm. Consequently, there is a requirement to include information about responding appropriately to a friend's self-harm in mental health education programmes.

- *Promoting school connectedness:* Schools with a high level of connectedness with its pupils, including good teacher–pupil relationships, good school environment and increased pupil engagement, appear to have less incidence of self-harm amongst students (Young et al., 2011).
- *Preventing bullying:* Many studies have identified the relationship between bulling at school and adolescent self-harm and suicidal behaviour (O'Connor et al., 2010). The development and implementation of a school bullying policy and an anti-bullying ethos is required for the provision of a safe environment for students.

Responding to a suicide in the school setting

A suicide within the school setting is a devastating occurrence for staff and students alike. The requirement to grieve for and remember the student who has died and also to reduce further suicidal behaviour and restore normal school functioning can be a difficult balance to strike. It is important to act quickly following the death of a student by suicide (or suspected suicide). Samaritans has developed a set of guidelines identifying several key considerations including:

- *Breaking the news:* Establish the facts. Notify management team and staff before notifying students. Break the news to students in small groups. When breaking the news be factual and avoid excessive detail about the suicidal act but be mindful that rumours may be circulating. Consider preparing a statement for staff to ensure consistency across the school. If appropriate, arrange counselling for staff and students.
- *Handling the media:* Depending on the particular circumstances, there may be media enquiries to the school. Appoint one person to liaise with media as necessary and discourage staff and students from making further comments. Avoid giving details of the suicide method or speculating about possible motives behind the suicide.
- *Contacting the school community:* The wider school community including parents may need to be informed about how the school is responding to the suicide and what action the school is taking to support students.
- *Communicating sensitively and appropriately about suicide:* Information imparted about the suicide should be factual without giving specific details and should not glorify or vilify the death. Information on sources of support and help should also be provided.
- *Identifying and supporting vulnerable students:* Teachers who know students best should identify any young people they feel are particularly vulnerable, or who appear excessively distressed by the death, as they may require additional support.
- *Memorials:* It is natural for students and staff to wish to remember the person who has died; however, it is also important not to glamorise or

sensationalise the suicide which may act as a trigger for anyone who is deeply affected. Permanent memorials following a suicide are generally discouraged.

■ *Funerals:* The nature of the student's death should not encourage greater attendance at the funeral than for any other student death. Ideally, students who attend the funeral should be accompanied by a parent/caregiver while those who do not wish to attend should have the option of attending class.

(Samaritans, 2013)

CASE SCENARIO 10.2

Laura is a 17-year-old post-primary student in her final year of school. Her parents have recently separated and she and her brother are living with their mother. She is very close to her father and has taken her parents separation very badly. Her final exams are approaching, and although Laura is a committed student who studies hard, she is excessively anxious about the exams and fears she will not perform as she would like to. As her teacher, you notice that her mood has been down for the past number of weeks. Whilst normally very attentive in class she now seems to be distracted and seems to have difficulty in concentrating. While walking past her desk during a class exam, you notice that Laura has deep and what seem to be recent scratches on her right arm. You are also aware that her best friend in school has self-harmed in the past.

■ What factors might have influenced Laura's self-harming behaviour?
■ How would you approach the issue of self-harm with Laura?
■ How can Laura be best supported in the school environment?

Self-harm and suicide in the Emergency Department

The Emergency Department (ED) is often the first port of call for those who have attempted suicide or have engaged in serious self-harm. Indeed, for many people the ED is the *only* healthcare setting they come into contact with after self-harm as a relatively large number of people are not referred on for specialised mental health services while a significant minority will leave the ED before being formally assessed. It is therefore critical that the person's experience in the ED and the interactions they have with staff there is positive. However, this is not always the case. It has been well documented that staff in EDs often do not feel skilled to adequately care for people who have self-harmed (Doyle et al., 2007). As a result their understanding of self-harm and suicidal behaviour is often poor which in turn has an effect on their attitudes towards those who have self-harmed.

Negative attitudes including feelings of irritation, anger and frustration towards those who self-harm are found to be most pronounced in the general medical setting, including the ED (Saunders et al., 2012). These feelings are associated with a number of factors including the perception that those who self-harm take valuable clinical time and resources away from those who are seen to have a more 'legitimate' reason for presenting to the ED. Frustration is often rooted in a feeling of helplessness, and these feelings along with other negative attitudes are more prevalent when people present with repeated self-harm (Gibb et al., 2010). In some situations, staff can be seen to make a value judgement on the 'genuineness' of a suicide attempt with more favourable care being received by those who are perceived to have made a more serious attempt at suicide (Doyle et al., 2007).

The sometimes negatives attitudes of ED staff is easily picked up on by those who have self-harmed. A systematic review of the attitudes of those who self-harm towards clinical services demonstrated that those who self-harmed believed that they were treated differently to other patients within the ED setting (Taylor et al., 2009). There was also the perception that ED staff focused only on the physical presentation and were unconcerned with their mental health. When asked to identify ways to improve interactions between those who self-harm and ED staff, participants suggested that staff needed to be more empathetic, less judgemental and have a better understanding of self-harm and the reasons that people engage in self-harm (Taylor et al., 2009). It is clear that there is potential for improvement of understanding and attitudes towards those who engage in self-harm within the ED. The ED is an important gateway to other services, both medical and mental health, and staff within the ED have an important role in reducing repeated self-harm and preventing suicide. However, the most basic starting point is understanding, empathy and respect for the person they are working with in order to help improve their outcomes and avoid a negative experience which may result in the service-user avoiding the ED for future episodes of self-harm with potentially serious consequences.

Responding to self-harm and suicidal behaviour within the Emergency Department

This section which focuses on how staff should respond to self-harm within the ED has drawn largely upon the NICE short-term management of self-harm guidelines (National Collaborating Centre for Mental Health, 2004). These guidelines identify a number of important steps in the short-term care of those presenting with self-harm including:

Triage: the staff member in the ED responsible for triage should assess the person's physical risk, cognitive function and mental capacity, and the person's emotional and mental state. The emotional distress the person is experiencing may be obvious; however, it may also be hidden and not outwardly exhibited. At the triage stage, there should also be a preliminary psychosocial assessment which should determine the person's mental capacity, their level of distress and their willingness to stay for a more depth psychosocial assessment. Although the person undertaking triage will not be carrying out an in-depth psychosocial assessment, they will require certain knowledge and competencies to carry out this initial psychosocial assessment and research suggests that ED nurses may not feel adequately prepared for this role (Keogh et al.,

2007). Therefore training in the management of self-harm is required for those working in the ED. This preliminary psychosocial assessment may also include an initial risk assessment to help determine the person's risk of further self-harm behaviour which may help establish the level of urgency for further psychosocial assessment and intervention. Risk assessment scales are often used in the determination of risk and are used frequently in EDs due to the increased pressure and demands placed on staff there. However, if utilised, these scales should only comprise *part of* a wider clinical assessment as they may not paint the full picture. An evaluation of the use of the SADPERSONS scale, used not infrequently in EDs, showed that it had a high false negative rating and in most cases failed to identify those requiring further mental health intervention and those who went on to engage in further self-harm (Saunders et al., 2013), thus demonstrating the dangers of using such scales in isolation. Following triage, if the person has to wait until they are seen for further treatment, they should be located in a safe, supportive environment in an attempt to minimise distress and to keep them safe from further self-harm. There should be regular contact with a staff member to avoid the feeling of isolation and to decrease the risk of the person leaving before further treatment.

Physical treatment: physical treatment should be carried out in an atmosphere of respect and understanding. Detailed information on the medical and surgical management of self-harm can be found in the NICE guidelines referenced above. Taylor et al. (2009) identified how people who self-harmed have had negative experiences of physical treatment in the ED including threats to withhold analgesia while suturing lacerations. This reflects a lack of understanding of self-harm and the functions that self-harm has for different people. The NICE guidelines suggest that adequate anaesthesia or analgesia be offered to people who have self-harmed throughout the process of suturing or other painful treatments.

Comprehensive Psychosocial assessment: The NICE guidelines recommend that all people presenting to the ED following self-harm have a comprehensive psychosocial assessment. However, on many occasions this does not occur as a significant proportion of people who present following self-harm leave after initial triage and a further proportion leave following physical treatment not having had a psychosocial assessment. This psychosocial assessment does not need to wait until physical treatment is complete unless the physical treatment required is urgent. When a detailed psychosocial assessment is carried out in the ED, it is often carried out by a mental health professional, usually a mental health liaison nurse or a mental health liaison psychiatrist. The NICE guidelines recommend that this assessment should comprise both an assessment of needs and a more detailed risk assessment than the one carried out in triage. The assessment of needs should include an evaluation of the social, psychological and motivational factors specific to the act of self-harm, current suicidal intent and hopelessness, as well as a full mental health and social needs assessment. The risk assessment should have an emphasis on determining the main clinical and demographic characteristics associated with self-harm/suicide and identification of the key psychological characteristics associated with risk including depression, hopelessness and high suicidal intent.

Referral for further services: Bilen et al. (2014) in their study found that those who attended the ED for treatment of self-harm and who were offered and attended follow up with specialised mental health services had a reduced risk of repeated self-harm. Specialised mental health services may take the form of the traditional mental health team led by a consultant psychiatrist or it could take the form of assertive outreach where the person is seen by a mental health professional (often a nurse) within a relatively short time period following discharge. However, not all those who present with self-harm require follow up with mental health services. The decision to refer service users to mental health services should be based on the assessment of risk and need carried out by the mental health professional and should be made in consultation with the service user. In addition to referring to specialised mental health services, the ED can act as a gateway to other services including counselling, family support, addiction services and social services. All decisions regarding referral of the person should be documented in the person's case notes and relayed to the person's GP and any relevant mental health service provider to facilitate speedy follow up if required.

CASE SCENARIO 10.3

Anna is a 27-year-old woman who has presented alone to the ED following self-inflicted wounds on her forearms. She smells strongly of alcohol and appears to be intoxicated. The scars are deep and will require sutures. Anna had previously cut her arms when she was a teenager; however, this occasion is different as the wound is much deeper than her previous superficial cuts. Anna is very distressed and has disclosed that her girlfriend of four years had ended their relationship without warning. She says that she finds it difficult to think of a future without her. The ED is very busy and after triage Anna is assigned to a noisy and full waiting room where she is told there will be a wait time of approximately three hours. While in the waiting room, Anna is observed to be increasingly distressed and agitated and appears to be contemplating leaving the ED.

- What factors should be considered in the initial psychosocial assessment in Triage?
- How might knowledge of Anna's previous self-harm impact on her assessment and care on this occasion?
- How might you respond to Anna's increasing distress and agitation?

Conclusion

This chapter has outlined some specific issues regarding self-harm and suicide in prisons, schools and emergency departments. It is evident from this chapter that working with those who engage in self-harm and suicidal behaviour is not solely the preserve of mental health professionals, but is a role undertaken by workers in a variety of different contexts. Understanding self-harm and suicide and knowing how to respond in an empathetic and human way to someone in distress is key to ensuring better outcomes for those who engage in suicidal behaviour. In addition, it is also crucial that workers in settings outside of mental health know how and when to refer people to specialised mental health services to prevent and/or manage an escalation of self-harm and suicidal behaviour.

REFERENCES

Best, R. (2005) An educational response to deliberate self-harm: Training, support and school-agency links. *Journal of Social Work Practice*, 19(3): 275–287.

Bilen, K., Pettersson, H., Owe-Larsson, B., Ekdahl, K., Ottosson, C., Castren, M. and Ponzer, S. (2014) Can early follow-up after deliberate self-harm reduce repetition? A Prospective study of 325 patients. *Journal of Affective Disorders*, 152(154): 320–325.

Doyle, L., Keogh, B. and Morrissey, J. (2007) Caring for patients with suicidal behaviour: An exploratory study. *British Journal of Nursing*, 16(19): 1218–1222.

Fazel, S, Grann, M., Kling, B. and Hawton, K. (2011) Prison suicide in 12 countries. *An ecological study of 861 suicides during* 2003–2007, 46: 191–195.

Gibb, S.J., Beautrais, A.L. and Surgenor, I.J. (2010) Health-care staff attitudes towards self-harm patients. *Australian and New Zealand Journal of Psychiatry*, 44: 713–720.

Hawton, K., Linsell, L., Adeniji, T., Sariaslan, A. and Fazel, S. (2014) Self-harm in prisons in England and Wales: An epidemiological study of prevalence, risk factors, clustering, and subsequent suicide. *The Lancet*, 383(9923): 1147–1154.

Hawton, K., Rodham, K. and Evans, E. (2006) *By Their Own Young Hand. Deliberate Self-Harm and Suicidal Ideas in Adolescents*. London: Jessica Kingsley Publishers.

Humber, N., Hayes, A., Senior, J., Fahy, T. and Shaw, J. (2011) Identifying, monitoring and managing prisoners at risk of self-harm/suicide in England and Wales. *The Journal of Forensic Psychiatry & Psychology*, 22(1): 22–51.

Keogh, B. Doyle, L. and Morrissey, J. (2007) Suicidal behaviour: A study of emergency nurses' educational needs when caring for this patient group. *Emergency Nurse*, 15(3): 30–35.

Lake, A.M. and Gould, M.S. (2011) School-based strategies for youth suicide prevenion. In O'Connor. R.C., Platt, S. and Gordon, J. (eds.) *International Handbook of Suicide Prevention. Research, Policy and Practice*. West Sussex: Wiley-Blackwell. pp 507–530

Liebling, A. (1992) *Suicide in Prison*. London: Routledge.

Madge, N., Hewitt, A., Hawton, K., de Wilde, E.J., Corcoran, P., Fekete, S, van Heeringen, K., De Leo, D. and Ystgaard, M. (2008) Deliberate self-harm within an international community sample of young people: Comparative findings from the Child & Adolescent Self-harm in Europe (CASE) Study. *The Journal of Child Psychology and Psychiatry*, 49(6): 667–677.

Marzano, L., Adler, J.R., and Ciclitira, K. (2013) Responding to repetitive, non-suicidal self-harm in an English male prison: Staff experiences, reactions and concerns. *Legal and Criminological Psychology*. doi: 10.1111/lcrp.12025.

National Collaborating Centre for Mental Health (2004) *Clinical Guideline 16. Self-harm: the Short Term Physical and Psychological Management and Secondary Prevention of Self-harm in Primary and Secondary Care*. London: National Institute for Clinical Excellence.

O'Connor, R.C., Rasmussen, S. and Hawton, K. (2010) *Northern Ireland Lifestyle and Coping Survey: Final Report*.http://www.dhsspsni.gov.uk/ni-lifestyle-and-coping-survey-2010.pdf

Patton, J. and Borrill, J. (2005) Prisons. In Duffy, D. and Ryan, T. (eds.) *New Approaches to Preventing Suicide: A Manual for Practitioners*. London: Jessica Kingsley Publishers.

Samaritans. (2013) *Help When We Needed it Most: How to Prepare and Respond to Suicide in Schools*. Surrey: Samaritans.

Saunders, K., Brand, F., Lascelles, K. and Hawton, K. (2013) The sad truth about the sadpersons Scale: An evaluation of its clinical utility in self-harm patients. *Emergency Medicine Journal*, 2013 Jul 29. doi: 10.1136/emermed-2013-202781.

Saunders, K.A.E., Hawton, K., Fortune, S. and Farrell, S. (2012) Attitudes and knowledge of clinical staff regarding people who self-harm: A systematic review. *Journal of Affective Disorders*, 139: 205–216.

Shaffer, D., Garland, A., Vaeland, V., Underwood, M.M, and Busner, C. (1991) The impact of curriculum-based suicide prevention program for teenagers. *Journal of the American Academy of Child and Adolescent Psychiatry*, 30: 588–596.

Taylor, T.L., Hawton, K., Fortune, S. and Kapur, N. (2009) Attitudes towards clinical services among people who self-harm: Systematic review. *British Journal of Psychiatry*, 194: 104–110.

Young, R., Sweeting, H. and Ellaway, A. (2011) Do schools differ in suicide risk? The influence of school and neighbourhood on attempted suicide, suicidal ideation and self-harm among secondary school pupils. *BMC Public Health*, 11: 874. http://www.biomedcentral.com/1471-2458/11/874.

Zahl, D.L. and Hawton, K. (2004) Repetition of deliberate self-harm and subsequent suicide risk: Long term follow-up study of 11,583 patients. *British Journal of Psychiatry*, 185: 70–75.

Index

Note: The letter 't' following locators refers to tables in the text.